WHAT THE FEAR IS GOING ON

Copyright © 2024

All rights are reserved, and no part of this publication may be reproduced, distributed, or transmitted in any manner, whether through photocopying, recording, or any other electronic or mechanical methods, without the explicit prior written permission of the publisher. This restriction applies to any form or means of reproduction or distribution.

Exceptions to this rule include brief quotations that may be incorporated into critical reviews, as well as certain other noncommercial uses that are allowed by copyright law. Any such usage must adhere to the specified conditions and permissions outlined by the copyright holder.

KJV:
Scriptures quoted from The Holy Bible:
King James Version. Thomas Nelson, 1987.

MSG:
Scriptures quoted from Peterson, Eugene H. The Message:
The Bible in Contemporary Language. NavPress, 2002.

NKJV:
Scriptures quoted from The Holy Bible:
New King James Version. Thomas Nelson, 1982.

Contents

01. A FORCE CALLED FEAR 4
02. FEAR ISN'T LOUD 16
03. THE IMPACT OF FEAR 35
04. WHEN GREAT PEOPLE FEAR 49
05. SPIRITUAL WARFARE: WHAT'S YOUR NAME? 66
06. CONFRONTING HIDDEN FEARS 91
07. FEAR OF THE UNKNOWN 103
08. FEAR OF REJECTION 121
09. FEAR OF LOSS 141
10. FEAR OF ISOLATION 171
11. FEAR OF SUCCESS 190
12. DO IT SCARED, BUT FEARLESS! 203

CHAPTER 1
A FORCE CALLED FEAR

2 Timothy 1:7
7 For God hath not given us the spirit of fear; but of power, and of love, and of a sound mind.

Fear is a formidable force, often lurking in the shadows of our minds, whispering doubts and anxieties that can paralyze progress and stifle growth. In the realm of leadership, fear can manifest in myriad ways, hindering decision-making, stifling innovation, and shaping a culture of hesitation and uncertainty.

Fear is not merely a psychological or emotional response; it holds a profound spiritual significance that can shape our beliefs, behaviors, and interactions with the world. The spiritual force of fear delves into the deeper layers of human consciousness, tapping into primal instincts and existential uncertainties.

Fear as a Catalyst for Transformation: When confronted with fear, individuals often experience a profound shift in their perception of reality. This transformation can lead to introspection, self-discovery, and ultimately personal growth.

The Power of Fear in Faith and Belief Systems: Many religions and spiritual practices acknowledge the role of fear in shaping one's relationship with the divine. Fear can serve as a motivator for seeking solace, guidance, or protection from higher powers.

Fear as an Energy Source: In esoteric traditions, fear is seen as a potent energy that can be harnessed for magical or ritualistic purposes. By channeling fear into focused intention, practitioners believe they can manifest desired outcomes or protect themselves from harm.

Exploring the spiritual force of fear opens up a realm of possibilities for understanding human nature and the interconnectedness between mind, body, and spirit. By acknowledging the transformative power of fear, individuals can navigate their fears with greater awareness and resilience.

In the landscape of human experience, fear stands as a force, shaping our decisions, our relationships, and our very perception of the world around us. As leaders, we often find ourselves at the crossroads of fear and faith, our choices rippling out to affect not just our own lives, but the lives of those we lead and serve.

This book, is born from a lifetime of grappling with fear in its myriad forms. As an apostle and senior pastor of two churches, as well as a consultant in corporate America specializing in organizational leadership, I've witnessed firsthand the pervasive nature of fear and its profound impact on leadership across all sectors of society.

The Spiritual Nature of Fear

While many believe that fear originates from external circumstances, our journey will reveal a deeper truth: fear often awakens at the very core of our being—our spirit. The Apostle Paul, in his letter to Timothy, provides us with a crucial insight:

> *"For God has not given us a spirit of fear, but of power and of love and of a sound mind." (2 Timothy 1:7, NKJV)*

This verse doesn't deny the existence of fear; rather, it clearly states that God is not its author or originator. If God is not the source of this spirit of fear, then we must confront an uncomfortable truth: the seeds of fear are sown by forces that stand in opposition to God's will.

Beyond the Fruits of Fear

Throughout this book, we will differentiate between the spirit of fear and its many fruits. Anxiety, worry, indecision—these are not the root of our struggles, but rather the visible manifestations of a deeper spiritual issue. By addressing only these symptoms, we find ourselves caught in an endless cycle of temporary relief and recurring distress.

Instead, we will dive deep into the nature of fear itself:

- Identifying the spiritual essence of fear
- Exploring its name and nature in biblical and spiritual contexts
- Developing strategies to combat the spirit of fear at its source
- Understanding how this spirit manifests in our physical and emotional experiences

The Ripple Effect of a Leader's Fear

As leaders, our relationship with fear extends far beyond our personal experience. The decisions we make, influenced by fear or faith, create ripples that touch the lives of all those under our care and authority. Whether in a church congregation, a corporate boardroom, or a community organization, the fear that governs a leader's heart inevitably finds its way into the culture and experiences of those they lead.

In the chapters that follow, we will explore:

- How fear manifests in tangible ways, affecting our hearts and minds
- The impact of a leader's fear on organizational culture and decision-making
- Practical and spiritual methods to overcome fear and lead with confidence

- Techniques for cultivating an environment of faith and courage within our spheres of influence

This work is not just about personal transformation—though that is where it begins. It is a call to leaders across all sectors to recognize, confront, and overcome the spirit of fear. By doing so, we can lead with greater clarity, confidence, and positive impact, empowering those we serve to step out of the shadows of fear and into the light of faith.

Fear as a Derailer of God's Purpose

Fear, when left unchecked, can act as a powerful force that derails individuals from fulfilling their divine purpose. It has the potential to cloud judgment, distort perceptions, and hinder one's ability to align with God's will. When fear takes hold, it can lead individuals down paths of doubt, insecurity, and disobedience, straying them away from the path that God has set before them. One of the primary ways in which fear derails God's purpose is by instilling a sense of inadequacy or unworthiness in individuals. When consumed by fear, individuals may doubt their abilities, question their worthiness to receive blessings or fulfill their calling. This self imposed limitation can prevent them from stepping into the fullness of their potential and embracing the opportunities that God has laid out for them.

Fear can also create barriers between individuals and their relationship with God. Instead of trusting in His guidance and providence, fear can lead to feelings of separation, distrust, or resentment towards God. This lack of faith and surrender can hinder individuals from fully experiencing the blessings and miracles that come from walking in alignment with His purpose.

Moreover, fear can manifest as resistance to change or growth. When faced with new challenges or opportunities for spiritual development, fear can cause individuals to retreat into familiar patterns or comfort zones out of a sense of security. This reluctance to embrace change and step into unknown territories can prevent them from evolving spiritually and fulfilling the unique purpose that God has ordained for them. In essence, fear acts as a derailer of God's purpose by sowing seeds of doubt, inadequacy, separation, and resistance within individuals. To overcome this obstacle and realign with God's will, it is essential for individuals to confront their fears head-on, cultivate faith in His plan, trust in His provision, and embrace growth with courage and conviction.

Unshaken: Nehemiah's Triumph Over Fear

In the annals of biblical history, few stories resonate with me as powerfully with the modern struggle against fear that tried to derail one from purpose as that of Nehemiah. As he embarked on the divine assignment to rebuild Jerusalem's walls, Nehemiah faced a barrage of threats designed to derail his mission. The Bible vividly recounts how Sanballat and Tobiah, adversaries to God's work, employed intimidation tactics to shake Nehemiah's resolve (Nehemiah 2:19-20, 4:1-3).

> 19 When Sanballat the Horonite, Tobiah the Ammonite official, and Geshem the Arab heard about it, they laughed at us, mocking, "Ha! What do you think you're doing? Do you think you can cross the king?"
>
> 20 I shot back, "The God-of-Heaven will make sure we succeed. We're his servants and we're going to work, rebuilding. You can stick to your own business. You get no say in this—Jerusalem's none of your business!"
>
> Nehemiah 2:19-20 (MSG)
>
> 4 1-2 When Sanballat heard that we were rebuilding the wall he exploded in anger, vilifying the Jews. In the company of his Samaritan cronies and military he let loose: "What are these miserable Jews doing? Do they think they can get everything back to normal overnight? Make building stones out of make-believe?"
>
> 3 At his side, Tobiah the Ammonite jumped in and said, "That's right! What do they think they're building? Why, if a fox climbed that wall, it would fall to pieces under his weight."
>
> Nehemiah 4:1-3 (MSG)

These threats, much like the whispers of doubt that plague our minds today, were arrows aimed at the heart of Nehemiah's purpose. They represent the spirit of fear that so often assails those called to significant work, whether in ministry of industry. This fear manifests as voices in our heads, painting bleak pictures of our future, attempting to pry us away from our divine assignments.

Yet, Nehemiah's response serves as a beacon of courage for all who face similar challenges. When invited to abandon his post under the guise of a meeting, Nehemiah's reply was resolute: "I am doing a great work and I cannot come down. Why should the work stop while I leave it and come down to you?" (Nehemiah 6:3, ESV). This declaration reveals a profound truth: Nehemiah's reverence for his work surpassed his fear of threats.

In this lies a powerful lesson for us all. To remain steadfast in our purpose, we must cultivate a deeper appreciation for our calling than for the fears that assail us. Nehemiah understood that the work of rebuilding Jerusalem's walls was not merely a physical task but a spiritual mandate. Similarly, our assignments, be they in ministry, business, or any other field, carry spiritual significance that transcends our immediate circumstances.

The key to plowing forward, undeterred by fear, lies in this realization: our work is greater than our fears. When we truly grasp the magnitude and importance of our God-given purpose, it becomes the anchor that holds us steady amidst the storms of doubt and intimidation. As Proverbs 29:25 (NIV) wisely states, "Fear of man will prove to be a snare, but whoever trusts in the Lord is kept safe."

Nehemiah's example challenges us to elevate our perspective. Instead of being cowed by threats or paralyzed by fear, we are called to fix our eyes on the higher purpose to which we've been called. This doesn't mean fear won't come; rather, it means we choose to press on despite it, knowing that our work serves a greater purpose.

In your own life, when faced with the arrows of fear—be they doubts about your abilities, concerns about the future, or threats from adversaries—remember Nehemiah. Let his unwavering commitment to his divine assignment inspire you to stand firm in your own calling.

For it is in continuing to build, even when our hands tremble, that we find the courage to complete the good work God has begun in us (Philippians 1:6).

Your purpose is too vital, your calling too significant, to be derailed by fear. Like Nehemiah, may you find the strength to declare, "I am doing a great work," and in that declaration, may you find the courage to continue, unshaken and undeterred.

Fear is Two-Faced: Every Leader Must Conquer

In the compelling narrative of Nehemiah's wall-building mission, we encounter a profound illustration of the dual nature of fear that leaders must confront. **Sanballat and Tobiah, Nehemiah's primary adversaries, serve as powerful prophetic representations of the two-pronged assault of fear on leadership: external threats and internal doubts.**

Sanballat: The Face of External Fear

Sanballat, whose name is thought to mean "sin has given life," embodies the external fears that leaders face. These are the visible obstacles, the tangible opposition, and the outward circumstances that threaten to derail our mission. In Nehemiah's case, Sanballat represented the political and social resistance to the rebuilding of Jerusalem's walls (Nehemiah 2:10, 4:1-2).

For modern leaders, Sanballat-type fears manifest as market challenges, competitive pressures, or public criticism. They are the fears that come from our environment, easily identified but often daunting in their apparent power.

Tobiah: The Whisper of Internal Fear

Conversely, Tobiah, whose name ironically means "Yahweh is good," represents the more insidious internal fears. These are the doubts that whisper in the quiet of our minds, the inherited insecurities passed down through generations, and the soul ties that bind us to past failures or limitations.

Internal fears, like Tobiah's subtle manipulations (Nehemiah 6:17-19), work from within. They exploit our vulnerabilities, playing on our deepest insecurities about our worthiness, capability, or right to lead. Statistics often reveal that most fears are indeed internal, making them perhaps the more formidable foe.

The Dual Battlefront of Leadership

Nehemiah's story teaches us that effective leadership requires vigilance on both fronts. We must not only steel ourselves against the external challenges that threaten our vision but also confront the internal doubts that undermine our resolve.

1. **Battling External Fears**: This involves developing strategies to overcome visible obstacles, building resilience against criticism, and maintaining focus amidst distractions. It's about standing firm in the face of opposition, much like Nehemiah positioning guards and rallying his people (Nehemiah 4:13-14).
2. **Conquering Internal Fears**: This deeper battle requires self-reflection, emotional intelligence, and often, spiritual warfare. It involves breaking generational cycles of fear, healing from past traumas, and severing unhealthy soul ties that keep us bound to limiting beliefs. Nehemiah exemplified this through his constant prayer and unwavering faith in God's purpose (Nehemiah 1:5-11, 2:4).

The Key to Total Victory

The crucial lesson from Nehemiah's experience is that true victory requires triumph on both battlefronts. As leaders, we may successfully overcome external challenges, but if we remain captive to our internal fears, our victory remains incomplete. Conversely, we may achieve inner peace and confidence, but if we fail to address external threats, our mission can still be compromised.

Nehemiah's success came from his ability to simultaneously address both dimensions of fear. He fortified the walls (external) while also strengthening the people's faith and resolve (internal). This dual approach ensured not just the completion of the wall but a transformative victory that renewed the entire community.

For leaders today, whether in ministry or industry, the message is clear: **acknowledge and confront both your Sanballats and your Tobiahs. Develop strategies to overcome external obstacles while also doing the inner work to address personal doubts and inherited fears.** Remember, as Proverbs 28:1 (NIV) states, "The righteous are as bold as a lion." This boldness comes from victory over both internal and external fears.

By waging and winning the war on both fronts, leaders can achieve a comprehensive victory—one that not only accomplishes the mission at hand but also transforms the leader and those they lead. In doing so, we follow in Nehemiah's footsteps, building not just walls, but legacies of fearless, purposeful leadership.

A Leaders Weapons Against Fear: Power, Love, and a Sound Mind

As we conclude our exploration of Nehemiah's battle against fear, we find a profound illustration of leadership that resonates across time, applicable in ministry, industry, and corporate America alike. Nehemiah's success in rebuilding Jerusalem's walls amidst fierce opposition offers us a blueprint for leadership that conquers fear through the divine gifts of power, love, and a sound mind.

Power: The Strength to Persist

Nehemiah's power was not derived from political authority or physical might, but from his unwavering faith and determination. This power manifested in several key ways:

1. **Decisive Action**: When faced with threats, Nehemiah didn't hesitate. He armed the builders (Nehemiah 4:13), demonstrating that power often lies in proactive measures.

2. **Empowerment of Others**: He encouraged the people, saying, "Don't be afraid of them. Remember the Lord, who is great and awesome" (Nehemiah 4:14 NIV). True power in leadership multiplies when shared.
3. **Persistence**: Despite constant opposition, Nehemiah persevered. The walls were completed in just 52 days (Nehemiah 6:15), a testament to the power of focused determination.

For modern leaders, this kind of power translates to having the courage to make tough decisions, the ability to inspire and empower team members, and the resilience to persist in the face of setbacks.

Love: The Heart of Leadership

Love might seem out of place in a discussion about battling fear, but Nehemiah's story reveals it as a crucial element:

1. **Compassion for His People**: Nehemiah's entire mission was driven by love for his people and heritage (Nehemiah 1:4-11). This love fueled his courage and commitment.
2. **Unity in Diversity**: He brought together people from various backgrounds to work towards a common goal (Nehemiah 3), showcasing love's power to unify.
3. **Servant Leadership**: Nehemiah led by example, working alongside the people and even funding the work from his own resources (Nehemiah 5:14-19).

In today's leadership landscape, love manifests as genuine care for team members, commitment to a greater purpose beyond profit, and the cultivation of an inclusive, supportive organizational culture.

A Sound Mind: The Foundation of Wise Leadership

Nehemiah's sound mind was evident in his strategic thinking and emotional intelligence:

1. **Strategic Planning**: Before even beginning the work, Nehemiah carefully assessed the situation and developed a plan (Nehemiah 2:11-16).
2. **Discernment**: He quickly recognized the schemes of his enemies and refused to be baited into traps (Nehemiah 6:1-4).
3. **Emotional Regulation**: Despite intense pressure, Nehemiah maintained his composure, making rational decisions rather than reacting out of fear.

For leaders today, a sound mind involves critical thinking, the ability to remain calm under pressure, and the wisdom to discern truth from deception in an age of information overload.

The Synergy of Power, Love, and a Sound Mind

The true genius of Nehemiah's leadership, and the lesson for us all, lies in how these three elements worked in concert:

- **Power without love** can become tyrannical, but Nehemiah's power was always tempered by his deep care for his people.
- **Love without a sound mind** can lead to poor decisions, but Nehemiah's affection for his nation was always guided by strategic thinking.
- **A sound mind without power** may result in good ideas never executed, but Nehemiah's wisdom was always backed by decisive action.

In the modern context, whether leading a ministry, steering a corporation, or innovating in industry, the interplay of these three elements is crucial:

- Use your **power** to make bold moves and empower others.
- Let **love** guide your purpose and foster a culture of unity and mutual support.
- Employ a **sound mind** to strategize effectively and navigate complex challenges.

Conclusion: Fearless Leadership in Any Arena

Nehemiah's story teaches us that fear – be it from external threats like Sanballat or internal doubts like those represented by Tobiah – can be overcome through the cultivation and application of power, love, and a sound mind. These are not just theological concepts but practical tools for effective leadership.

In your own leadership journey, whether you're building literal walls like Nehemiah or metaphorical ones in your organization, remember:

1. Stand in your God-given power, taking decisive action and empowering others.
2. Lead with love, fostering unity and serving those you lead.
3. Maintain a sound mind, thinking strategically and discerning wisely.

By embodying these principles, you can, like Nehemiah, lead fearlessly, inspire greatly, and accomplish what others deem impossible. In doing so, you not only achieve your goals but also leave a legacy of courageous, compassionate, and wise leadership that stands the test of time.

CHAPTER 2
FEAR ISN'T LOUD

John 8:44
You belong to your father, the devil, and you want to carry out your father's desires. He was a murderer from the beginning, not holding to the truth, for there is no truth in him. When he lies, he speaks his native language, for he is a liar and the father of lies.

Fear, when left unchecked, has the insidious ability to manifest as a whisperer of lies in the minds and hearts of individuals. It subtly weaves a web of deceit, distorting reality and feeding individuals with false narratives that undermine their confidence, faith, and sense of purpose. These whispers of fear can take on various forms, from subtle doubts to outright falsehoods that erode one's trust in themselves and in God. One way fear acts as a whisperer of lies is by planting seeds of doubt in individuals' minds. It convinces them that they are not capable, worthy, or deserving of God's blessings and guidance. These insidious whispers can lead individuals to question their abilities and worthiness, creating barriers that prevent them from stepping into their divine purpose with confidence and conviction.

Moreover, fear can distort perceptions and create false narratives about one's relationship with God. It may whisper lies about God's intentions, His love for His children, or His plans for their lives. These deceptive whispers can breed feelings of separation, distrust, or resentment towards God, further alienating individuals from His grace and guidance. Furthermore, fear as a whisperer of lies can fabricate stories about the future, instilling anxiety and uncertainty in individuals' hearts. It may paint bleak scenarios or worst-case outcomes that paralyze individuals with fear and prevent them from embracing change or growth. These false narratives hinder spiritual evolution and block individuals from aligning with the path that God has laid out for them. In essence, fear manifesting as a whisper of lies undermines individuals' faith, distorts their perceptions, and hinders their ability to walk in alignment with God's purpose. To combat these deceptive whispers, it is crucial for individuals to confront their fears with truth, seek clarity through prayer and reflection, and anchor themselves in unwavering faith in God's promises and providence.

The Whisper of Fear: Unmasking Its Subtle Influence

In the cacophony of leadership challenges, fear often emerges not as a roar, but as a whisper. It's a subtle intruder, slipping past our defenses through the voices of those we trust, aiming to silence the confident timbre of our leadership voice.

The Anatomy of Fear

Examine the word 'fear' closely, and you'll find 'ear' nestled within its letters. This linguistic curiosity reveals a profound truth: fear requires our ear to fulfill its insidious mission. It's not merely a coincidence of spelling, but a stark reminder of how fear operates.

Fear is an opportunist, always listening for an opening, waiting for a moment of vulnerability to whisper its debilitating message. **It understands that to paralyze a leader, it need not shout; it only needs to be heard.**

The Trojan Horse of Applause

Beware the Trojan horse of effusive praise. There are those who will applaud you loudly in public, their claps echoing with seeming support, while in private moments, they lean in close to whisper seeds of doubt into your heart. **These individuals are particularly** dangerous because their outward support lowers your defenses, making you susceptible to their whispered fears.

"You're doing great, but are you sure you're ready for this level of responsibility?" "The team loves you, but can you really handle the pressure when things get tough?" "Your vision is inspiring, but do you think it's a bit too ambitious?"

These whispers, cloaked in concern and delivered by trusted voices, can be far more damaging than outright criticism. They plant the seeds of self-doubt that, if nurtured, can grow into forests of fear, obscuring your path and purpose.

Guarding Your Ear, Guarding Your Heart

As leaders, we must develop a discerning ear — one that can distinguish between constructive feedback and fear-inducing whispers. This discernment is crucial because not all soft-spoken words are harmful, and not all loud praises are genuine.

1. **Evaluate the Source**: Consider the track record of the person speaking. Do their words typically uplift and challenge you positively, or do they often leave you feeling uncertain and diminished?
2. **Check the Timing**: Be wary of "concerns" raised just before significant decisions or important events. Fear often strikes when it can have the maximum impact.
3. **Assess the Aftermath**: After hearing their words, do you feel empowered to act or paralyzed with doubt? True support, even when challenging, should ultimately strengthen your resolve.
4. **Trust Your Inner Voice**: Cultivate a strong connection with your inner wisdom. Often, your gut instinct can distinguish between legitimate concerns and fear-based manipulations.
5. **Seek Multiple Perspectives**: Don't rely on a single source of feedback. Cultivate a diverse circle of advisors who can offer balanced perspectives.

From Whisper to Roar: Transforming Fear

The ultimate triumph over fear's whisper is to acknowledge it, understand it, and then use it as fuel. When you recognize fear's attempt to infiltrate through your ear, you can choose to transform it. Let the whisper of fear become the roar of your determination.

Remember, as a leader, your voice has power. While fear seeks to quiet you, your role is to speak vision, hope, and direction loudly and clearly. By guarding your ear against fear's whisper, you protect your ability to speak boldly into the lives of those you lead.

In the end, leadership is not about the absence of fear-inducing whispers, but about ensuring that your voice – the voice of courage, vision, and purpose – resonates more powerfully than any whisper of doubt. Let your leadership be a beacon that drowns out the shadows of fear with the light of possibility and progress.

The Whisper of Lies: Fear's Assault on Leadership Identity

In the intricate dance of leadership, fear often takes the lead in the most insidious way - through the whisper of lies. These lies, when internalized, can transform a leader from a beacon of truth into an unwitting propagator of falsehoods. This descent into deception is not merely a moral failing but a strategic move by the enemy of our souls to derail divine purpose.

The Anatomy of Fear's Deception

The Bible clearly states that the devil is the father of lies (John 8:44). His modus operandi is to weave intricate webs of deceit, designed to entangle leaders and drag them away from the truth of their identity. This strategy is particularly potent because it targets the very core of leadership - authenticity and integrity.

When fear whispers lies into the ears of leaders, it seeks to:

1. Distort self-perception

2. Undermine confidence in one's calling
3. Breed mistrust in God's promises
4. Encourage compromise of values
5. Foster a culture of secrecy and shame

The end goal is clear: to bring leaders out of alignment with their true identity in the kingdom of God, rendering them ineffective or, worse, counterproductive to their divine mandate.

King David: Lies and Leadership

The life of King David provides a compelling case study of how lies, born of fear, can entangle even the most anointed of leaders. David, described as a man after God's own heart (Acts 13:22), was not immune to the whisper of lies. Let's examine key moments where lies threatened to derail his leadership:

1. The Lie of Unworthiness

When faced with Goliath, David had to contend not just with the giant, but with the lies spoken by his own brother and the lies spoken by the giant: "I know how conceited you are and how wicked your heart is" (1 Samuel 17:28, NIV). This lie attacked David's identity and sought to disqualify him from his calling.

This epic confrontation has long served as a metaphor for overcoming seemingly insurmountable odds. However, beneath the surface of this tale lies a profound truth often overlooked: the battle doesn't end when the giant falls.

The Visible Victory

The moment the stone from David's sling found its mark, and Goliath crashed to the ground, a visible victory was won. The Philistine champion, who had terrorized the Israelite army with his imposing presence and booming voice, lay silent. In that instant, David transformed from a shepherd boy to a national hero.

This external triumph is what we often celebrate. It's tangible, visible, and immediate. The giant is slain, the threat neutralized, and the day is won. But is the battle truly over?

The Invisible Battle

What we fail to realize is that while David silenced Goliath's voice, the echo of the giant's words continued to reverberate in his mind. The seeds of doubt, fear, and inadequacy that Goliath had sown remained, taking root in the fertile soil of David's consciousness.

Consider the taunts David faced:

- "Am I a dog, that you come at me with sticks?" (1 Samuel 17:43)
- "Come here, and I'll give your flesh to the birds and the wild animals!" (1 Samuel 17:44)

These weren't merely empty threats. They were calculated attacks on David's identity, capability, and worth. Even after Goliath's defeat, these lies lingered, whispering doubts:

- "Was it just luck?"
- "Can you live up to this moment?"
- "Are you truly worthy of leading?"

The Dual Nature of Victory

True victory, then, is twofold. It requires us to:

1. **Slay the Giant**: Confront and overcome the external challenges, the visible opponents that stand in our way.
2. **Slay the Lie**: Identify and uproot the internal falsehoods, the invisible doubts that take residence in our minds.

David's journey post-Goliath illustrates this struggle. Despite his monumental victory, he faced moments of doubt, fear, and insecurity throughout his life. His psalms often reflect this internal battle:

- "My God, my God, why have you forsaken me?" (Psalm 22:1)

- "I am a worm and not a man, scorned by everyone, despised by the people." (Psalm 22:6)

These words reveal that even after slaying the giant, David grappled with the lies that questioned his worth and God's presence in his life.

Strategies for Slaying the Lie

To achieve complete victory, we must be as intentional about confronting internal lies as we are about facing external giants. Here are strategies to slay the lie:

1. **Identify the Lie**: Recognize the false narratives that have taken root in your mind. What negative self-talk persists even after your victories?

2. **Confront the Source**: Trace the lie back to its origin. Was it planted by a critic, a past failure, or societal expectations?

3. **Speak Truth**: Counter each lie with truth. David did this by reminding himself of God's faithfulness: "The Lord who rescued me from the paw of the lion and the paw of the bear will rescue me from the hand of this Philistine." (1 Samuel 17:37)

4. **Seek Wise Counsel**: Surround yourself with truth-tellers who can help you discern between fact and fiction in your self-perception.

5. **Celebrate Small Victories**: Acknowledge and celebrate the times you choose truth over lies. Each small win reinforces your true identity.

6. **Renew Your Mind**: Regularly feed your mind with uplifting, truth-filled content. For David, this meant composing and singing psalms that reaffirmed God's goodness and his own calling.

The Ongoing Battle

Slaying the giant and the lie is not a one-time event but an ongoing process. Just as David faced many more battles after Goliath, we too will encounter new challenges and fresh lies throughout our journey. The key is to approach each one with the dual mindset of confronting both the external obstacle and the internal falsehood it might leave behind.

A Call to Complete Victory

As leaders, visionaries, and believers, we are called not just to external success but to internal freedom. Let us not be satisfied with merely silencing the voice of our opponents. Instead, let us pursue the complete victory that comes from slaying both the giant before us and the lie within us.

Remember, the stone that brings down the giant is courage, but the sword that slays the lie is truth. Wield both with precision, and watch as you achieve victories that are not just visible to the world but transformative to your soul.

In the words of David himself, let this be our battle cry: "I keep my eyes always on the Lord. With him in my right hand, I will not be shaken." (Psalm 16:8)

Slay the giant, then slay the lie. This is the path to true, lasting victory.

2. The Lie of Self-Preservation

In a moment of fear, David lied to Ahimelech the priest about his mission, leading to tragic consequences (1 Samuel 21:1-2). This lie, born from the fear of Saul, showed how easily a leader can compromise truth when feeling threatened.

From Past Fears to Future Lies

In the journey of leadership, the shadows of our past often stretch long into our future, casting darkness over new opportunities and relationships. This truth is poignantly illustrated in the life of David, specifically in his interaction with Ahimelech the priest. This episode serves as a stark reminder that unresolved fears from previous seasons can compel us to live and propagate lies in the seasons to come.

The Echo of Past Fears

David's encounter with Ahimelech occurs as he's fleeing from Saul, a man who once mentored him but now seeks his life. In 1 Samuel 21:1-2, we read:

"David went to Nob, to Ahimelech the priest. Ahimelech trembled when he met him, and asked, 'Why are you alone? Why is no one with you?' David answered Ahimelech the priest, 'The king sent me on a mission and said to me, "No one is to know anything about the mission I am sending you on."'"

This lie, born from David's fear of Saul, would have devastating consequences. It led to the death of Ahimelech and 85 other priests (1 Samuel 22:18-19), marking one of the darkest chapters in David's journey.

The Cycle of Fear and Deception

David's actions reveal a painful truth: the fears of our 'Sauls' - past persecutors, traumas, or failures - can drive us to deceive the 'Ahimelechs' of our future - those who could be allies, supporters, or mentors in our next season. This cycle of fear leading to deception can:

1. Compromise our integrity
2. Damage new relationships before they have a chance to flourish
3. Sabotage opportunities for growth and advancement
4. Perpetuate a pattern of mistrust and isolation

The Vacancy of Unhealed Wounds

"Unhealed places are simple vacancies for lies to be released." This profound statement illuminates the danger of unresolved trauma and fear. Like a vacant home becomes a target for squatters, our unhealed wounds become breeding grounds for lies - lies about our worth, our safety, and our future.

These vacancies in our emotional and spiritual well-being create a vacuum that fear is all too eager to fill. In David's case, his unresolved fear of Saul created a vacancy that was quickly occupied by the lie he told Ahimelech.

Hearing the Damage Before Embracing Faith

Sometimes, we need to fully acknowledge and hear the extent of the damage fear has wrought in our lives before we can truly embrace faith for our future mission. This process of acknowledgment and healing is crucial for several reasons:

1. **It Breaks the Power of Denial**: Facing our fears and their consequences head-on removes their power to operate in the shadows of our subconscious.
2. **It Facilitates True Repentance**: Understanding the depth of damage caused by fear-driven actions leads to genuine remorse and a desire for change.
3. **It Opens the Door to Healing**: Acknowledging our wounds is the first step towards seeking and receiving healing.
4. **It Restores Perspective**: Seeing the full picture of fear's impact helps us realize the value of faith and truth in our lives.
5. **It Prepares Us for Future Challenges**: Learning from past mistakes equips us to face new seasons with greater wisdom and resilience.

Breaking the Cycle: From Fear to Faith

To move from a place of fear-driven deception to faith-filled leadership, consider these steps:

1. **Confront Your 'Sauls'**: Identify the past experiences, people, or traumas that still instill fear in you. Name them, face them, and begin the process of healing.
2. **Audit Your 'Vacancies'**: Take inventory of the unhealed places in your life. These are potential breeding grounds for lies and fear.
3. **Seek Healing Actively**: Engage in counseling, prayer, or whatever healing modalities align with your faith and values. Don't rush this process.

4. **Practice Radical Honesty**: Begin with small steps of truthfulness, even when it's uncomfortable. Build a reputation for integrity in minor matters.

5. **Cultivate Faith-Filled Relationships**: Surround yourself with 'Ahimelechs' who encourage your growth and speak truth into your life.

6. **Anchor in Your True Identity**: Regularly remind yourself of who you are in God's eyes, not in the shadow of your past fears.

7. **Learn to Discern**: Develop the ability to distinguish between genuine threats and echoes of past fears.

The Promise of a New Season

As leaders, we have the opportunity to break this cycle of fear and deception. By addressing our past, healing our wounds, and stepping out in faith, we can enter new seasons with integrity and hope. Remember, every 'Ahimelech' in your future deserves to encounter the true you, not a version shaped by past fears.

In the words of the Psalmist David, who eventually learned this lesson:

> "I sought the Lord, and he answered me; he delivered me from all my fears." - Psalm 34:4

Let this be the testimony of our leadership journey: not that we never knew fear, but that we allowed faith to triumph over it, ushering in seasons of truth, integrity, and purposeful mission.

3. The Lie of Invincibility

Perhaps the most dangerous lie David believed was that he was above reproach. This led to his affair with Bathsheba and the subsequent cover-up, including the murder of Uriah (2 Samuel 11). Here, we see how one lie can spiral into a web of deceit that threatens to destroy a leader's integrity and legacy.

You Are Not Beyond Reproach

In the pantheon of leadership pitfalls, few are as insidious and destructive as the lie of being beyond reproach. This deception, often born from a cocktail of success, fear, and unchecked power, can lead even the most promising leaders astray. King David's tragic affair with Bathsheba and the subsequent murder of Uriah serve as a stark biblical illustration of this dangerous mindset.

The Intoxication of Power

David, the shepherd boy turned king, had ascended to heights few could imagine. Anointed by God, victorious in battle, and beloved by his people, David might have felt invincible. This sense of invulnerability likely contributed to his belief that he could take Bathsheba for himself and dispose of her husband without consequences.

This lie – that he was beyond reproach – led David to commit grievous sins:

1. Adultery with Bathsheba (2 Samuel 11:4)
2. Attempted cover-up (2 Samuel 11:6-13)
3. The murder of Uriah (2 Samuel 11:14-17)

The Addiction to Living a Lie

When leaders begin to believe they're beyond correction, they often become addicted to living and telling lies. This addiction is fueled by:

1. **Fear of Vulnerability**: The terror of appearing weak or fallible
2. **Pride**: An inflated sense of self-importance
3. **Isolation**: Surrounding oneself with yes-men who never challenge
4. **Past Successes**: Using previous wins as a shield against current scrutiny

This addiction manifests in leadership behaviors such as:

- **Closed-Door Policies**: Shutting out dissenting voices and feedback
- **Authoritarian Leadership Styles**: "Do what I say, as I say, don't question me"
- **Resistance to Accountability**: Viewing any form of checks and balances as insubordination

The Illusion of Immunity

Leaders trapped in this lie often believe they're immune to:

1. **Criticism**: Viewing all critique as an attack rather than potential for growth
2. **Consequences**: Assuming their position shields them from repercussions
3. **Moral Standards**: Believing that the rules don't apply to them
4. **Divine Judgment**: Forgetting that even anointed leaders answer to a higher authority

The Reality of Consequences

David's story reminds us that no one, not even a king "after God's own heart," is beyond consequences. The repercussions of David's actions were severe:

- Death of the child born from the affair (2 Samuel 12:18)
- Rape of his daughter Tamar (2 Samuel 13:1-22)
- Murder of his son Amnon (2 Samuel 13:23-33)
- Rebellion of his son Absalom (2 Samuel 15-18)

These consequences, while not curses, were the natural outflow of David's actions rooted in the lie of being beyond reproach.

Breaking Free from the Lie

To avoid falling into this trap or to break free if already ensnared, leaders must:

1. **Cultivate Humility**: Remember that leadership is a responsibility, not a right
2. **Embrace Accountability**: Actively seek out and welcome constructive criticism
3. **Practice Transparency**: Foster an environment where honesty is valued over image
4. **Acknowledge Fallibility**: Admit mistakes quickly and sincerely
5. **Seek Wise Counsel**: Surround yourself with advisors who will speak truth to power
6. **Remember Your Mortality**: Recognize that all leaders, no matter how great, are human
7. **Stay Connected to Your Source**: For those of faith, maintain a vibrant relationship with God

The Power of Repentance

David's story doesn't end with his sin. When confronted by the prophet Nathan, David repented sincerely (Psalm 51). This act of humility and contrition allowed for:

1. Restoration of his relationship with God
2. Continued leadership, albeit with consequences
3. A powerful testimony that has inspired millions

A Call to Accountable Leadership

As leaders, we must vigilantly guard against the lie of being beyond reproach. Our position doesn't exempt us from accountability; rather, it demands an even higher standard of integrity.

Remember:

- Open doors invite growth; closed doors breed stagnation
- Welcome contention as an opportunity for refinement
- Embrace rebuke as a path to improvement
- View consequences not as curses, but as catalysts for change

In doing so, we create a leadership culture that is robust, resilient, and truly transformative. Let us lead not from a place of fearful self-protection, but from a position of humble strength, always ready to be refined by truth and accountable to those we serve.

4. The Lie of Abandonment

During Absalom's rebellion, David momentarily believed the lie that God had abandoned him, saying, "If I find favor in the Lord's eyes, he will bring me back to Jerusalem. But if he says, 'I am not pleased with you,' then I am ready; let him do to me whatever seems good to him" (2 Samuel 15:25-26, NIV). This lie struck at the heart of David's relationship with God.

From Abandonment to Engagement: Overcoming the Lie of Divine Desertion

In the tapestry of David's life, few threads are as dark and tangled as the period of Absalom's rebellion. This crisis not only threatened David's throne but also shook the very foundations of his faith and relationships. It serves as a powerful illustration of how the lies we believe can create a false sense of abandonment, distorting our view of God and affecting our ability to engage with the future.

The Seed of Abandonment

As Absalom's rebellion gained momentum, David found himself fleeing Jerusalem, his city, his throne, and seemingly, his destiny. In this moment of crisis, a lie took root in David's heart – the lie that God had abandoned him. We see this reflected in his words:

"But if he says, 'I am not pleased with you,' then here I am, let him do to me whatever seems good to him." (2 Samuel 15:26, NIV)

This statement reveals a profound shift in David's thinking. The man who once declared, "The Lord is my shepherd, I lack nothing" (Psalm 23:1), now entertained the possibility that God might be displeased with him to the point of abandonment.

The Lie's Ripple Effect

Once David began to entertain this lie of abandonment, it created a ripple effect in his life:

1. **Distorted View of God**: David started to see God not as a faithful protector, but as a fickle deity who might withdraw His favor.
2. **Strained Relationships**: His uncertainty about God's presence affected his interactions with others. We see this in his suspicious treatment of Mephibosheth (2 Samuel 16:1-4) and his initial acceptance of Shimei's curses (2 Samuel 16:11-12).
3. **Passive Leadership**: The lie of abandonment led David to a more passive approach to leadership. Instead of actively seeking God's guidance, he seemed to resign himself to whatever fate would bring.
4. **Emotional Turmoil**: Psalms believed to be written during this period (such as Psalm 3 and 63) reveal David's inner struggle with feelings of abandonment and his fight to hold onto faith.

The Dangerous Space of Yesterday's Lie

David's experience teaches us a crucial lesson: the lies we believe about yesterday can create dangerous spaces in our relationships tomorrow. When we internalize a false sense of abandonment, it can:

1. Make us hesitant to fully engage in new relationships
2. Cause us to misinterpret others' actions through a lens of expected rejection
3. Lead us to preemptively withdraw to protect ourselves from perceived future abandonment
4. Hinder our ability to trust and fully commit to new opportunities

Overcoming False Abandonment

To move from a place of perceived abandonment to full engagement with the future, we must:

1. **Recognize the Lie**: Acknowledge that our sense of abandonment may be based on a false narrative, not reality.
2. **Reaffirm God's Character**: Remind ourselves of God's faithful nature. As David eventually did, we must declare, "But you, Lord, are a shield around me, my glory, the One who lifts my head high." (Psalm 3:3)
3. **Seek Counsel**: Surround ourselves with wise advisors who can provide perspective when our vision is clouded by lies.
4. **Practice Active Faith**: Instead of passively accepting our circumstances, actively seek God's guidance and move forward in faith.
5. **Renew Relationships**: Make conscious efforts to engage fully in relationships, choosing vulnerability over self-protection.
6. **Learn from the Past Without Being Bound by It**: Use past experiences as lessons, not as predictors of future outcomes.

The Path to Re-engagement

David's story doesn't end in abandonment. Despite his momentary doubt, he eventually reclaims his throne and his confidence in God's presence. This journey from perceived abandonment to re-engagement is marked by:

1. Renewed prayer and worship (Psalm 63)
2. Acceptance of support from others (2 Samuel 17:27-29)
3. Strategic action aligned with faith (2 Samuel 17:1-14)
4. Mercy and reconciliation (2 Samuel 19:9-15)

A Call to Future-Focused Leadership

As leaders, we must be vigilant against the lie of abandonment. Our past experiences, no matter how painful, do not dictate God's presence in our future. The spaces created by yesterday's lies can become fertile ground for tomorrow's faith if we choose to:

1. Continuously renew our understanding of God's unchanging nature

2. Engage fully in present relationships and opportunities
3. Lead from a place of active faith rather than passive acceptance
4. Use our experiences of overcoming to inspire and guide others

In doing so, we not only reclaim our own destiny but also create a legacy of resilient, faith-filled leadership that inspires generations to come. Let us, like David, move from the shadow of perceived abandonment into the light of full engagement with the future God has prepared for us.

Breaking Free from the Entanglement of Lies

Despite these moments of faltering, David's legacy as a great leader remains intact. His ability to break free from the entanglement of lies offers valuable lessons for leaders today:

1. **Embrace Vulnerability**: David's psalms show his willingness to be honest about his struggles, fears, and failings before God and others.
2. **Pursue Truth Relentlessly**: Even when confronted with his sins, David sought the truth, no matter how painful (2 Samuel 12:1-13).
3. **Return to Identity**: David consistently returned to his identity as God's chosen, finding strength and courage in this truth.
4. **Practice Repentance**: When entangled in lies, David modeled sincere repentance, allowing God to restore him to his true identity (Psalm 51).
5. **Speak Truth to Power**: David surrounded himself with people like Nathan, who were willing to speak truth, even when it was difficult to hear.

The Leader's Mandate: Living in Truth

As leaders, our calling is not to perfection, but to authenticity. The antidote to fear's whispered lies is the bold proclamation of truth - truth about who we are in God's kingdom, truth about our struggles and victories, and truth about the unfailing nature of God's promises.

When we choose to live in truth, we not only safeguard our own leadership but also create an environment where others can flourish in their authentic identities. In doing so, we transform the whisper of lies into a resounding chorus of truth that echoes through our spheres of influence, advancing the kingdom of God with integrity and power.

Remember, every lie believed is a temporary victory for fear, but every truth embraced is an eternal victory for the kingdom. As leaders, let us commit to being vigilant guardians of truth, in our lives and in the lives of those we lead.

CHAPTER 3
THE IMPACT OF FEAR

Imposter Syndrome in Leadership

Imposter syndrome is a psychological phenomenon where individuals doubt their accomplishments and have a persistent fear of being exposed as a fraud. In the context of leadership, imposter syndrome can have significant implications on how leaders perceive themselves, make decisions, and interact with their teams. One of the key impacts of imposter syndrome on leaders is a lack of confidence in their abilities. Leaders experiencing imposter syndrome may constantly second-guess their decisions, hesitate to take risks, and feel unworthy of their position. This self-doubt can hinder their effectiveness in leading teams, making strategic choices, and inspiring confidence among their followers.

Moreover, imposter syndrome can lead to a fear of failure that paralyzes leaders from taking necessary actions or pursuing ambitious goals. The constant fear of being exposed as incompetent or inadequate can prevent leaders from stepping out of their comfort zones, innovating, or embracing challenges that could lead to growth and success for themselves and their organizations.

Another consequence of imposter syndrome in leadership is the tendency to downplay achievements or attribute success to external factors rather than acknowledging one's own skills and capabilities. This reluctance to take credit for accomplishments can undermine a leader's credibility, diminish team morale, and create a culture where self-doubt is normalized instead of celebrating achievements. To overcome imposter syndrome in leadership, it is essential for individuals to cultivate self-awareness, seek support from mentors or coaches, challenge negative self-talk, and reframe perceptions of success and failure. By addressing these underlying beliefs and fears, leaders can build resilience, boost confidence, and lead with authenticity and conviction.

The Spirit of Imposter Syndrome: Fear's Assault on Divine Purpose

In the intricate tapestry of leadership challenges, few threads are as insidiously woven as imposter syndrome. This spirit of fear, which whispers lies of inadequacy and fraudulence, has a particular affinity for those walking in divine purpose. Like a skilled counterfeiter, it creates an authentic-looking replica of humility while actually manufacturing a paralysis of purpose.

The Paradox of Divine Appointment

When God appoints a leader, He does so with full knowledge of their capabilities, shortcomings, and potential. Yet, ironically, those most firmly planted in their divine purpose often face the fiercest battles with imposter syndrome. This is no coincidence – it's a strategic spiritual attack designed to neutralize effective leadership before it reaches its full potential.

Consider Moses at the burning bush: "Who am I that I should go to Pharaoh and bring the Israelites out of Egypt?" (Exodus 3:11) Even with a literal divine encounter, the spirit of imposter syndrome attempted to grip his heart through fear.

The Anatomy of Leadership Imposter Syndrome

The spirit of imposter syndrome in leadership operates through several key mechanisms:

1. **Distortion of Divine Calling**
    - Questions the authenticity of God's appointment

- Magnifies human inadequacy while minimizing divine enablement
- Creates a false separation between the called and the Caller

2. **Manipulation of Memory**
   - Minimizes past successes
   - Amplifies past failures
   - Reframes God's previous faithfulness as coincidence or luck

3. **Paralysis of Present Purpose**
   - Breeds hesitation in decision-making
   - Fosters over-dependence on external validation
   - Creates a constant state of second-guessing

4. **Fear of Future Exposure**
   - Generates anxiety about being "found out"
   - Instills dread of future challenges
   - Plants seeds of doubt about sustained success

The Assignment of Fear

The spirit of imposter syndrome has a specific assignment in leadership:

1. **To Create Distance**
   - Between the leader and their calling
   - Between the leader and their confidence
   - Between the leader and their community

2. **To Induce Isolation**
   - Making leaders feel uniquely inadequate
   - Preventing vulnerable conversations about struggles
   - Discouraging authentic leadership connections

3. **To Prevent Progress**
   - By fostering analysis paralysis

- Through excessive self-doubt
- Via continuous second-guessing

4. **To Maintain Bondage**
   - To past failures
   - To others' opinions
   - To perfectionist standards

The Grip on the Heart

Imposter syndrome grips the heart through fear in several ways:

1. **Fear of Inadequacy** "Who am I to lead?" "What if I'm not qualified enough?" "Do I really have what it takes?"
2. **Fear of Discovery** "What if people realize I'm not as capable as they think?" "What if my weaknesses become exposed?" "What if I can't maintain this level of leadership?"
3. **Fear of Future Failure** "What if I make a crucial mistake?" "What if I let everyone down?" "What if I'm not ready for the next challenge?"

Breaking the Grip: Spiritual Strategies for Victory

To overcome the spirit of imposter syndrome, leaders must:

1. **Realign with Divine Perspective**
   - Remember God's calling is not based on human qualification
   - Focus on God's strength rather than personal inadequacy
   - Embrace the truth that His power is made perfect in weakness (2 Corinthians 12:9)
2. **Recognize the Attack**
   - Identify imposter syndrome as a spiritual assault
   - Understand its patterns and triggers
   - Call it out for what it is: fear masquerading as humility

3. **Reclaim Authority**
   - Stand firm in your divine appointment
   - Speak truth over lies
   - Exercise spiritual authority over fear

4. **Rebuild Community**
   - Share struggles with trusted mentors
   - Connect with other leaders
   - Create safe spaces for vulnerability

The Path to Authentic Leadership

True leadership, empowered by divine purpose, must:

1. **Embrace Imperfection**
   - Acknowledge that God's calling includes our weaknesses
   - Use vulnerability as a strength
   - Allow grace to perfect our leadership

2. **Exercise Faith Over Fear**
   - Choose to believe God's word over internal doubts
   - Act decisively despite feelings of inadequacy
   - Trust in divine enabling rather than human capability

3. **Engage in Continual Growth**
   - View challenges as opportunities for development
   - Maintain a learning posture
   - Celebrate progress over perfection

A Call to Courageous Leadership

Remember: The presence of imposter syndrome often indicates you're precisely where God wants you to be. The enemy doesn't waste resources attacking inconsequential targets. Your battle with feeling like an impostor might be the strongest evidence that you're authentically walking in your purpose.

Let us therefore lead:

- Not from a place of perfectionism, but purpose
- Not from fear of exposure, but faith in our calling
- Not from doubt in our abilities, but trust in His enabling

For it is precisely in our acknowledgment of inadequacy that God's adequacy shines brightest. In embracing our humanity while leaning on His divinity, we find the sweet spot of authentic, purposeful leadership.

Decision Paralysis: When Fear Freezes Leadership

The Paralysis of Two Opinions

> *"How long will you halt between two opinions? If the LORD be God, follow him: but if Baal, then follow him." (1 Kings 18:21)*

This powerful moment on Mount Carmel reveals a fundamental truth about leadership and decision-making: indecision is not neutrality—it is surrender to fear. The Israelites' silence in response to Elijah's challenge wasn't wisdom or prudence; it was paralysis born of fear.

The Conception of Fear in Decision-Making

Fear breeds in the womb of uncertainty, growing through these stages:

1. **Initial Doubt**
    - Questions arise about potential outcomes
    - Multiple scenarios create confusion
    - Past failures cast shadows on future choices

2. **Analysis Overwhelm**
   - Over-processing of information
   - Endless seeking of more data
   - Perpetual need for confirmation

3. **Emotional Escalation**
   - Anxiety about making the wrong choice
   - Fear of consequences
   - Dread of responsibility

4. **Decision Paralysis**
   - Complete inability to move forward
   - Frozen between options
   - Stuck in a cycle of overthinking

The Cost of Not Deciding

"Not making a decision is still making a decision." This truth reveals the hidden damage of decision paralysis:

1. **Spiritual Costs**
   - Delayed obedience becomes disobedience
   - Faith becomes stagnant
   - Divine timing is missed

2. **Leadership Costs**
   - Team momentum is lost
   - Trust in leadership erodes
   - Vision becomes blurry

3. **Organizational Costs**
   - Opportunities slip away
   - Resources are wasted
   - Competition gains advantage

4. **Personal Costs**
   - Confidence diminishes
   - Stress accumulates
   - Leadership credibility suffers

The Anatomy of Decision Paralysis

Fear manifests in decision-making through several key mechanisms:

1. **The Perfectionism Trap**
   - Waiting for perfect conditions
   - Seeking impossible guarantees
   - Demanding complete certainty

2. **The Analysis Loop**
   - Endless research
   - Perpetual consultation
   - Continuous re-evaluation

3. **The Responsibility Dodge**
   - Diffusing decision-making to committees
   - Seeking unnecessary consensus
   - Avoiding personal accountability

4. **The Fear Factor**
   - Fear of failure
   - Fear of criticism
   - Fear of success

Biblical Patterns of Paralysis

Scripture provides several examples of decision paralysis and its consequences:

1. **The Israelites at the Red Sea**
   - Paralyzed between advancing and retreating
   - Required divine intervention
   - Learned faith through crisis

2. **The People Under Saul**
   - Frozen in fear of Goliath
   - Waited for someone else to act
   - Lost opportunities for victory

3. **The Church at Laodicea**
   - Neither hot nor cold
   - Comfortable in indecision
   - Lost effectiveness in purpose

Breaking Free from Decision Paralysis

1. **Embrace Divine Guidance** "Trust in the LORD with all your heart and lean not on your own understanding." (Proverbs 3:5)
   - Seek God's wisdom first
   - Trust biblical principles
   - Follow peace in decision-making

2. **Establish Decision Frameworks**
   - Set clear decision criteria
   - Create timeline boundaries
   - Define non-negotiables

3. **Accept Imperfect Progress**
   - Recognize that some movement is better than none
   - Understand that course corrections are normal
   - Value learning through action

4. **Develop Decision Momentum**
   - Start with smaller decisions
   - Build confidence through action
   - Celebrate progress over perfection

The Power of Decisive Leadership

Leaders must understand that:

1. **Decision-Making is Stewardship**
   - Time is a finite resource
   - Opportunities have expiration dates
   - Influence requires action

2. **Movement Creates Clarity**
   - Action reveals hidden obstacles
   - Progress provides new perspective
   - Motion generates momentum

3. **Faith Requires Action**
   - Trust is demonstrated through movement
   - Obedience often precedes understanding
   - Growth comes through stepping out

Practical Steps for Overcoming Decision Paralysis

1. **Set Decision Deadlines**
   - Establish clear timeframes
   - Create accountability structures
   - Honor commitment to action

2. **Implement Decision Filters**
   - Mission alignment check
   - Values consistency review

- Resource capacity assessment

3. **Develop Response Protocols**
   - Emergency decision procedures
   - Routine decision frameworks
   - Strategic decision processes

The Call to Decisive Leadership

As leaders, we must recognize that:

1. **Indecision is a Decision**
   - It's choosing to let circumstances decide
   - It's surrendering leadership influence
   - It's abdicating responsibility

2. **Movement Requires Courage**
   - Faith to step forward
   - Strength to face uncertainty
   - Boldness to lead change

3. **Decision-Making is Growth**
   - Each decision builds capacity
   - Every choice creates learning
   - All movement produces maturity

Let us remember that the opposite of fear isn't always courage—sometimes it's simply action. In leadership, the willingness to decide, to move, to act, even imperfectly, often proves more valuable than waiting for perfect conditions or complete certainty.

The leader's call is not to always make perfect decisions, but to make timely ones, rooted in wisdom, guided by faith, and executed with conviction. For in the economy of leadership, a timely "good" decision often proves more valuable than a delayed "perfect" one.

The Weight of Yesterday's Fear: My Journey Through Decision Paralysis

I remember sitting in my office, staring at that email – the one that would confirm my acceptance of a CFO position. My finger hovered over the mouse, frozen in that familiar space of paralysis I had come to know so well. The promotion would mean leading a large team, requiring open-door policies, one-on-one mentoring sessions with my accounting staff, and the kind of vulnerability I had spent years carefully avoiding.

In these moments, my mind always drifts back to when I was twelve, when trust became a weapon and safety became an illusion. My cousin, a frequent person I was around at my grandmother's house, a "trusted" family member, stole more than just my innocence – he stole my ability to trust my own judgment. Violation comes with manipulative assurances that this is your "special thing," or you call it "little secret." These moments of confusion will crystallize into a pattern of doubt that would infiltrate every significant decision in the life of an adult.

"What if I can't protect myself?" I whispered to my empty office. "What if I can't protect them?"

The promotion wasn't the only decision haunting me. There was also an unanswered text from a woman I'd been dating for three months. She was kind, patient, and understanding – everything my counselor had helped me identify as healthy relationship traits. Yet her invitation to deepen our relationship through premarital counseling sat unanswered, joining my growing collection of relationship milestones I'd frozen in front of.

The pattern was familiar to me now: Any situation requiring vulnerability triggered an avalanche of "what-ifs." What if my judgment was wrong again? What if trust was just another trap? What if vulnerability invited violation? These questions would swirl until the opportunity passed, adding another regret to my growing collection of unmade decisions.

As a man, and particularly as a Black man in leadership, I faced additional layers of complexity in dealing with my trauma. Society's expectations of masculine strength, combined with cultural stigmas around both male victimhood and mental health, had initially made it harder to acknowledge my struggles. For years, I channeled my pain into overachievement, building walls of accomplishments behind which I could hide my wounds.

My counselor helped me understand that my hypervigilance and decision paralysis weren't signs of weakness – they were my childhood self's survival mechanisms functioning overtime. That young boy had learned that trust could be weaponized, that closeness could harbor danger, and that his "no" could be ignored. In response, I developed an elaborate system of checks and balances for every decision, especially those involving trust and vulnerability.

But that day felt different. I reached for the journal my counselor had suggested I keep. Opening to a fresh page, I wrote:

"The fears that paralyze me were born in moments I didn't choose. But my future doesn't have to be held hostage by my past. Every decision I make today is a reclamation of my power to choose, my right to lead, and my ability to create safe spaces for others."

I looked at the words, feeling their weight and truth. My past had taught me to fear vulnerability, but it had also given me an incredible gift – the ability to recognize genuine safety and authentic relationships. My hesitation wasn't weakness; it was wisdom waiting to be balanced with courage.

Taking a deep breath, I began to type a reply to my girlfriens: "I want to take this step with you. Can we talk about what this counseling journey might look like and how we can make it feel safe for both of us?" My heart raced as I pressed send, but there was also a surge of quiet pride. This wasn't just a response to a text – it was a declaration that my past trauma would no longer have the final say in my future connections.

Turning back to the promotion email, I felt the familiar fear rise up. But this time, I acknowledged it differently: "I see you, fear. I understand why you're here. But you're a reminder of my past, not a prediction of my future."

With that thought, I clicked "Accept."

Later that evening, as I packed up my office, I noticed something had shifted. The decisions I'd made hadn't eliminated my fear or erased my past, but they had demonstrated something powerful: my ability to feel fear without letting it have the final word. Each choice to move forward, even with trembling steps, was a victory over the paralysis that trauma had tried to make my permanent home.

I added one final line to my journal entry:

"Healing doesn't mean never being afraid. It means learning to walk with fear without letting it choose your path. Every decision made in spite of fear is a step toward reclaiming not just choice, but the beautiful vulnerability that makes authentic leadership and genuine relationships possible. My story, my pain, and my healing journey can create spaces for others to find their courage too."

I share this deeply personal story because I know I'm not alone in this struggle. For those of you walking through your own valleys of decision paralysis, especially those carrying the weight of past violations, I want you to know that the path forward isn't about eliminating fear or doubt. It's about learning to make space for courage alongside them. Each decision, each step toward vulnerability, is both an act of healing and a reclamation of power.

Our traumas may have taught us to doubt, but they also gave us incredible gifts – sensitivity, discernment, and the ability to create safe spaces for others. These aren't weaknesses to overcome, but strengths to be channeled into our leadership and relationships.

Today, I still face moments of paralysis, but I've learned to see them differently. They're not just obstacles to overcome; they're opportunities to demonstrate that while our past experiences may inform us, they don't have to define us. Every decision we make in spite of fear is a testament to the healing power of courage and the strength found in vulnerable leadership.

CHAPTER 4
WHEN GREAT PEOPLE FEAR

In examining fear-based patterns through a biblical lens, we find numerous instances where individuals grappled with fear and its consequences. From Adam and Eve hiding in shame after disobeying God to Moses doubting his ability to lead the Israelites out of Egypt, fear has been a recurring theme in the Bible. One notable example is the story of Gideon, who initially doubted his worthiness and capabilities when called by God to lead the Israelites against their enemies. Despite his fears, Gideon eventually found courage and strength through faith, demonstrating that overcoming fear is possible with trust in God's guidance.

Similarly, King David faced many challenges that could have instilled fear in him, yet he repeatedly turned to God for strength and courage. In Psalm 27:1, David declares, "The Lord is my light and my salvation—whom shall I fear? The Lord is the stronghold of my life—of whom shall I be afraid?" This verse highlights the power of faith in dispelling fear and finding refuge in God's protection. Furthermore, Jesus' teachings often addressed the issue of fear, encouraging his followers not to be anxious about tomorrow but to trust in God's provision. In Matthew 6:34, Jesus says, "Therefore do not worry about tomorrow, for tomorrow will worry about itself. Each day has enough trouble of its own." This reminder emphasizes the importance of living in the present moment without succumbing to fear or anxiety about the future. By exploring these biblical narratives and teachings on fear-based patterns, we gain insights into how faith can help individuals overcome their fears and insecurities. Just as biblical figures found strength in trusting God's plan despite their doubts and uncertainties, modern-day leaders can draw inspiration from these stories to confront their fears with faith and resilience.

Born for Greatness, Battling Generational Fear: Breaking Inherited Chains

The Paradox of Destined Greatness

When the angel of the Lord appeared to Gideon, he declared, "The Lord is with you, mighty warrior" (Judges 6:12). Yet at that very moment, Gideon was threshing wheat in a winepress, hiding from the Midianites. This paradoxical scene perfectly illustrates how destiny and fear can coexist in the same vessel. Here was a man chosen for greatness, appointed for victory, yet crouching in the shadows of his own apprehension.

The Inheritance of Fear

Gideon's response to his divine calling reveals the depth of his inherited fear: "Pardon me, my lord, but how can I save Israel? My clan is the weakest in Manasseh, and I am the least in my family" (Judges 6:15). This wasn't just personal doubt – it was the voice of generational inadequacy speaking through him.

The Anatomy of Generational Fear

1. **Family Narrative**
    - "My clan is the weakest..."
    - "I am the least..."
    - Words that become prophetic limitations
    - Stories that shape identity

2. **Inherited Patterns**
    - Fear passing from parent to child
    - Survival mechanisms becoming family traits

- Limitation becoming legacy
- Doubt becoming DNA

3. **Environmental Conditioning**
   - Growing up in an atmosphere of fear
   - Learning to hide one's potential
   - Adopting a mindset of scarcity
   - Inheriting a posture of survival

The Manifestation of Generational Fear

Gideon's story reveals how generational fear manifests in several ways:

1. **Identity Distortion**
   - Seeing yourself through the lens of family limitation
   - Defining your potential by past failures
   - Carrying the weight of ancestral defeat
   - Believing in inherited inadequacy

2. **Behavioral Patterns**
   - Hiding from opportunity
   - Seeking excessive confirmation
   - Doubting divine appointment
   - Minimizing personal capacity

3. **Spiritual Blockages**
   - Questioning God's choice
   - Doubting divine promises
   - Requiring repeated signs
   - Struggling with trust

Breaking the Generational Cycle

God's interaction with Gideon provides a blueprint for breaking generational fear:

WHAT THE FEAR IS GOING ON

1. **Divine Declaration**
   - "The Lord is with you, mighty warrior"
   - Identity established before victory
   - Destiny spoken over doubt
   - Purpose proclaimed over past

2. **Progressive Challenges**
   - Starting with the family altar (Judges 6:25-27)
   - Moving to community impact
   - Scaling to national deliverance
   - Each step building faith

3. **Pattern Interruption**
   - Breaking family idols
   - Challenging community norms
   - Establishing new traditions
   - Creating fresh legacies

The Journey from Fear to Faith

Gideon's transformation teaches us vital lessons about overcoming generational fear:

1. **Acknowledge the Source**
   - Recognize inherited fears
   - Name family patterns
   - Identify root causes
   - Accept the reality of generational impact

2. **Embrace Divine Identity**
   - Accept God's declaration over family definition
   - Choose heaven's perspective over historical limitation
   - Allow new truth to overwrite old lies

- Build identity on promise, not past

3. **Take Progressive Steps**
    - Start with personal altars
    - Move to family transformation
    - Extend to community impact
    - Advance to destiny fulfillment

The Power of Breaking Generational Fear

When Gideon finally broke free from generational fear, the impact was multi-generational:

1. **Personal Victory**
    - From hiding to leading
    - From doubt to decisiveness
    - From fear to faith
    - From weakness to warrior

2. **Family Transformation**
    - Breaking idolatrous patterns
    - Establishing new traditions
    - Creating legacy of courage
    - Shifting family narrative

3. **National Impact**
    - Delivering Israel
    - Inspiring others
    - Creating new history
    - Establishing precedent of victory

Greatness in the Face of Fear

The truth remains: greatness does not exempt us from battles with fear. Instead, it often magnifies them. But like Gideon, we must understand that:

1. **Fear's Presence Doesn't Negate Calling**
   - Destiny remains despite doubt
   - Purpose persists through panic
   - Calling continues through confusion
   - Anointing abides amid anxiety

2. **Family History Isn't Final Destiny**
   - Past patterns can be broken
   - New legacies can be created
   - Fresh narratives can be written
   - Divine destiny can override family dysfunction

3. **Victory Is Progressive**
   - Each step builds strength
   - Every win weakens fear's grip
   - Small acts of courage lead to major breakthroughs
   - Today's bravery becomes tomorrow's breakthrough

A Call to Destined Greatness

For every leader battling generational fear while carrying a mantle of greatness, remember:

1. Your destiny is not diminished by your struggles with fear
2. Your family history is a chapter, not the conclusion
3. Your inherited fears can become platforms for supernatural victory
4. Your breakthrough can become generational blessing

Like Gideon, you may have inherited fear, but you were born for greatness. The very presence of fear in your life may be the strongest indicator that your destiny threatens the enemy's plans. Your calling isn't just about personal victory – it's about breaking chains that have bound generations and establishing a new legacy of faith-filled leadership for generations to come.

Let the truth echo in your spirit: You can be both chosen for greatness and challenged by fear. The key is not the absence of fear, but the presence of faith that moves forward despite it. Your destiny is greater than your doubt, and your calling is stronger than your concerns.

In the end, like Gideon, you may find that the very fears you inherited become the platform for displaying God's power and establishing a new generational legacy of courage and victory.

Rejecting Another Man's Chains: Breaking Free from Borrowed Bondage

The Weight of Another Man's Armor

When David stood before Saul, preparing to face Goliath, the king did what seemed logical – he offered the young shepherd his own armor. "Then Saul dressed David in his own tunic. He put a coat of armor on him and a bronze helmet on his head" (1 Samuel 17:38). This moment represents more than just an ill-fitting suit of armor; it symbolizes how authority figures often pass down their own protection mechanisms, their fears, and their limitations to the next generation.

David's response was profound: "I cannot go in these... I am not used to them" (1 Samuel 17:39). In these words, we find a revolutionary declaration of freedom from inherited chains. David understood something crucial – wearing another man's armor, or carrying another man's chains, would hinder rather than help his destiny.

The Chains We Never Forged

Like hand-me-down clothes that never quite fit, we often wear the constraints, fears, and limitations of the men who came before us. These chains clank with familiar sounds:

1. **The Echo of a Father's Fear**
   - His unresolved trauma
   - His abandoned dreams
   - His patterns of escape
   - His religious bondage

2. **The Weight of a Leader's Wounds**
   - Previous pastor's betrayals
   - Their unfinished battles
   - Their compromised values
   - Their limited vision

3. **The Burden of Bloodline Battles**
   - Generational curses
   - Family dysfunction
   - Cultural limitations
   - Historical trauma

Saul's Armor: The Chains of Protection

Saul's armor represents different types of inherited chains:

1. **Physical Chains**
   - Methods that worked for others
   - Systems that protected them
   - Strategies they trusted
   - Defenses they built

2. **Psychological Chains**
   - Fear-based thinking
   - Limiting beliefs
   - Self-protective mechanisms
   - Risk-averse mindsets

3. **Spiritual Chains**
   - Religious traditions
   - Man-made restrictions
   - Borrowed battles
   - Inherited intimidations

The Danger of Wearing Another Man's Armor

Like David trying to walk in Saul's armor, wearing another man's chains can:

1. **Restrict Your Movement**
   - Limiting your unique expression
   - Hindering your natural gifts
   - Constraining your divine purpose
   - Slowing your progress

2. **Distort Your Identity**
   - Masking your authentic self
   - Confusing your calling
   - Blurring your boundaries
   - Compromising your confidence

3. **Delay Your Victory**
   - Complicating simple battles
   - Adding unnecessary weight
   - Creating artificial barriers

- Preventing divine strategy

David's Declaration: Rejecting Inherited Limitations

David's rejection of Saul's armor teaches us to:

1. **Trust Your Training**
   - Value your unique experiences
   - Honor your personal journey
   - Respect your natural abilities
   - Build on your proven victories

2. **Embrace Your Authenticity**
   - Walk in your own authority
   - Use your own weapons
   - Fight your own way
   - Trust your own calling

3. **Face Your Giants Unencumbered**
   - Remove limiting protection
   - Shed borrowed barriers
   - Release inherited fears
   - Stand in your own strength

Breaking Free from Borrowed Bondage

To break free, we must:

1. **Identify the Armor**
   - Recognize whose protection you're wearing
   - Understand how it limits you
   - Acknowledge its impact on your calling
   - See where it doesn't fit

2. **Remove the Chains**
   - Strip away inherited limitations
   - Shed generational fears
   - Release borrowed battles
   - Remove false protection

3. **Choose Your Own Weapons**
   - Select tools that fit your calling
   - Use methods that match your makeup
   - Employ strategies suited to your strength
   - Fight with faithful confidence

Creating a New Legacy

Once free, your responsibility becomes:

1. **Building New Systems**
   - Establishing healthy patterns
   - Creating life-giving cultures
   - Developing empowering environments
   - Forging fresh pathways

2. **Breaking Cycles**
   - Ending destructive patterns
   - Interrupting negative transfers
   - Preventing chain inheritance
   - Starting new traditions

3. **Blessing Future Generations**
   - Passing down freedom
   - Transferring truth
   - Conveying courage
   - Inspiring authenticity

The Power of Authentic Leadership

Like David, we must:

1. **Know Our True Identity**
   - Understand who God says we are
   - Trust our divine preparation
   - Value our unique journey
   - Honor our authentic calling

2. **Use Our Proven Weapons**
   - Build on personal experience
   - Trust God-given abilities
   - Apply tested strategies
   - Rely on genuine strengths

3. **Face Our Giants Our Way**
   - Confront challenges authentically
   - Apply divine wisdom personally
   - Trust God's specific leading
   - Walk in individual anointing

A Declaration of Freedom

Let it be declared:
- You are not required to wear another man's armor
- You are not responsible for another man's battles
- You are not bound by another man's limitations
- You are not defined by another man's failures

Your assignment is to:

1. Remove what restricts you
2. Release what isn't yours
3. Reclaim your authentic voice

4. Restore God's original design

The Promise of Victory

Like David, your greatest victories will come when you:

1. Reject ill-fitting protection
2. Trust your divine preparation
3. Use your proven weapons
4. Fight in faith and freedom

Remember: The armor you refuse today might be the chain you prevent from binding another tomorrow. Your courage to be authentic doesn't just free you – it liberates generations.

Stand firm in this truth: You were not born to wear another man's armor or bear another man's chains. You were born to break them, showing others the power of walking in their God-given identity and authority.

Running in His Shoes: Breaking My Father's Chain of Flight

There are moments in our lives that plant seeds so deep within our spirits that we don't recognize their fruit until years later. For me, that moment came in the form of footprints in the woods – my father's footprints, leading away from me.

I was just a child when my mother took me to meet him. The memory still plays like a slow-motion film: the anticipation building in my young heart, the weight of expectations hanging in the air, and then... the sight of a man running away into the woods. Running away from me. Running away from responsibility. Running away from love.

In my younger years, I developed an aversion to being called "li woo." The nickname stung not because it was inherently harmful, but because it tethered me to a man who chose

flight over fatherhood. What I didn't realize then was that I was wearing his shoes, running his race, carrying his chain.

The Inheritance of Flight

As I grew older, a pattern emerged in my life. When relationships deepened, I ran. When opportunities required commitment, I ran. When love demanded vulnerability, I ran. I had unknowingly slipped my feet into my father's running shoes, wearing them so long they felt like my own.

The chain of running manifested in various ways:
- Leaving situations before they could leave me
- Avoiding deep connections
- Creating distance in relationships
- Mastering the art of emotional escape
- Perfecting premature exits

I didn't realize I was running. I had convinced myself I was just "moving on," "being independent," or "avoiding complications." But in therapy, the truth emerged like a sunrise – slow, steady, and illuminating. I wasn't just running; I was running in my father's footsteps.

The Revelation of Inherited Chains

The moment of recognition in therapy was both painful and liberating. There I sat, a grown man, suddenly seeing the invisible chain I'd been dragging – a chain forged in those woods years ago. I was the manifestation of my father's flight, producing the fruit of his fear, perpetuating a cycle of running that began before I took my first step.

That revelation brought me to my knees, literally and figuratively. How many relationships had I run from? How many opportunities had I fled? How many beautiful moments had I missed because I was wearing shoes meant for escape rather than embrace?

Taking Off the Running Shoes

Breaking this chain required more than recognition – it demanded action. I had to:

1. **Face the Pain**
    - Acknowledge the wound of abandonment
    - Feel the impact of that day in the woods
    - Name the pain of wearing another man's chains

2. **Understand the Pattern**
    - Identify my triggers for flight
    - Recognize my running mechanisms
    - Accept my inherited responses

3. **Choose to Stand**
    - Make conscious decisions to stay
    - Fight through the urge to flee
    - Build new patterns of presence

The Process of Breaking Free

Breaking free from this inherited chain meant:

1. **Removing the Shoes**
    - Consciously rejecting the pattern of running
    - Choosing to plant my feet firmly in my own identity
    - Creating new footprints of faithfulness

2. **Breaking the Chain**
    - Forgiving my father
    - Releasing the past
    - Creating new patterns

3. **Walking a New Path**
    - Staying present in discomfort

- Building lasting connections
- Embracing vulnerability

The Victory of Standing Still

Today, I stand as a man who has learned to:
- Face challenges instead of fleeing them
- Build relationships instead of running from them
- Create stability instead of seeking escape
- Choose presence over flight

A Message to Others Wearing Inherited Shoes

To those who recognize themselve he s in this story – those wearing shoes they didn't buy and running races they didn't choose – I say:

1. **You Can Stop Running**
   - The pattern can be broken
   - New paths can be formed
   - Different choices can be made

2. **You Can Stand Strong**
   - Your feet can find firm ground
   - Your heart can learn to stay
   - Your spirit can embrace stability

3. **You Can Create New Footprints**
   - For yourself
   - For your children
   - For generations to come

The Legacy of Standing

Now when I hear "li woo," it no longer carries the sting of inheritance. Instead, it reminds me of victory – of the day I

took off another man's running shoes and chose to stand, to stay, to be present.

My father may have run into those woods, but his chain of flight stopped with me. I chose to break the pattern, to remove the shoes, and to shatter the chain. And in doing so, I created a new legacy – one of standing firm, staying present, and choosing love over flight.

For those still running in inherited shoes, know this: You can stop. You can take them off. You can break the chain. The path of flight ends when you choose to stand – when you decide that your story will be different, that your legacy will be one of presence, not absence.

The woods of your past may hold the footprints of those who ran, but your future can hold the strong, steady stance of one who chose to stay.

CHAPTER 5
SPIRITUAL WARFARE: WHAT'S YOUR NAME?

Fear, though often overt and recognizable, can also manifest in subtle ways that may go unnoticed but still have a significant impact on an individual's thoughts and actions. Recognizing these subtle tactics of fear is crucial in addressing them effectively and breaking free from their grip. One common subtle tactic of fear is procrastination. When individuals delay taking action or making decisions out of fear of failure or rejection, they are allowing fear to control their behavior. By identifying procrastination as a potential sign of underlying fear, individuals can address the root cause and move forward with courage.

Another subtle tactic is perfectionism. Striving for unattainable standards or constantly seeking approval from others can stem from a deep-seated fear of not being good enough. Recognizing perfectionism as a mask for underlying fears allows individuals to embrace imperfection and cultivate self-compassion. Self-doubt is another insidious tactic that fear employs to undermine confidence and prevent individuals from stepping into their full potential. When negative self-talk or imposter syndrome creeps in, it is essential to recognize these thoughts as products of fear and challenge them with self-affirming beliefs. Comparison is yet another subtle tactic through which fear operates, leading individuals to measure their worth against others and fostering feelings of inadequacy or insecurity. By acknowledging comparison as a tool of fear, individuals can shift their focus inward, embracing their unique strengths and qualities without the need for external validation.

Recognizing the subtle tactics through which fear operates is key to overcoming its influence on our lives. By identifying procrastination, perfectionism, self doubt, and comparison as manifestations of underlying fears, individuals can take proactive steps to address these issues and reclaim control over their thoughts and actions.

Spiritual Warfare Against Fear: Unmasking the Spirit of Fear and Its Demonic Alliances

Understanding Fear's Identity

The spirit of fear operates with a specific identity - a name that reveals its nature and operation. Just as the Bible tells us that the name of the Lord is a strong tower (Proverbs 18:10), knowing the enemy's name gives us authority in spiritual warfare.

The Name and Nature of Fear

In Hebrew, one of fear's names is "Emah" (אֵימָה) "Immani", which connects to:

- Dread
- Terror
- Horror
- Overwhelming anxiety

Understanding this name reveals fear's:

- Operational patterns
- Points of entry
- Areas of influence
- Tactical approaches

The Demonic Alliance: Fear's Partnerships

The spirit of fear rarely operates alone. It partners with other spirits to create strongholds:

1. **Spirit of Confusion**
   - Clouds judgment
   - Distorts reality
   - Creates chaos in decision-making
   - Prevents clear thinking

2. **Spirit of Paralysis**
   - Freezes action
   - Prevents progress
   - Immobilizes purpose
   - Stifles movement

3. **Spirit of Doubt**
   - Questions God's faithfulness
   - Undermines faith
   - Challenges truth
   - Breeds uncertainty

4. **Spirit of Isolation**
   - Separates from community
   - Breaks relationships
   - Creates loneliness
   - Prevents accountability

5. **Spirit of Depression**
   - Dampens hope
   - Darkens perspective
   - Drains energy

- Diminishes joy

Weapons of Our Warfare

"For the weapons of our warfare are not carnal, but mighty through God to the pulling down of strong holds" (2 Corinthians 10:4)

1. **The Word of God**

Key Scriptures for Battle:

- "For God has not given us a spirit of fear, but of power and of love and of a sound mind" (2 Timothy 1:7)
  - Declare your divine equipment
  - Reject fear's legitimacy
  - Claim your sound mind
- "There is no fear in love; but perfect love casts out fear" (1 John 4:18)
  - Use love as a weapon
  - Allow perfect love to expel fear
  - Stand in God's love
- "When I am afraid, I put my trust in you" (Psalm 56:3)
  - Transform fear into faith
  - Make trust your default
  - Redirect focus to God

Strategic Prayer Points

Breaking Fear's Authority

"In the name of Jesus Christ, I break the authority of the spirit of fear over my life. I cancel its assignments, break its partnerships with confusion, paralysis, doubt, isolation, and depression. I declare that fear has no legal right to operate in my life or ministry."

Establishing Divine Order

"I establish the order of the Holy Spirit in my mind, emotions, and decisions. I declare that perfect love casts out all fear. I receive the spirit of power, love, and a sound mind."

Dismantling Strongholds

"I pull down every stronghold built by fear in my life. I demolish arguments and every pretense that sets itself up against the knowledge of God. I take captive every thought to make it obedient to Christ."

Practical Warfare Strategies

1. **Identify Fear's Entry Points**
   - Childhood trauma
   - Negative experiences
   - Inherited fears
   - Environmental influences

2. **Seal the Gates**
   - Apply the blood of Jesus
   - Establish boundaries
   - Build spiritual walls
   - Maintain vigilance

3. **Replace Fear's Tutoring**
   - Unlearn fear's lessons
   - Replace with truth
   - Establish new patterns
   - Build faith foundations

Leading Others to Freedom

As leaders, we must help others:

1. **Recognize Fear's Language**
   - Identify fear-based speech
   - Notice fear-driven behavior
   - Understand fear's mindset
   - Detect fear's influence

2. **Unlearn Fear's Curriculum**
   - Challenge fear's teachings
   - Question fear's assumptions
   - Reject fear's conclusions
   - Replace fear's lessons

3. **Establish New Patterns**
   - Create faith-based responses
   - Build courage muscles
   - Develop trust habits
   - Form new neural pathways

Warfare Declarations for Leaders

Authority Declaration

"As a leader appointed by God, I take authority over the spirit of fear affecting my sphere of influence. I declare freedom for those under my leadership."

Breaking Generational Patterns

"I break every generational covenant with fear. I cancel its effects on past, present, and future generations in my lineage and leadership."

Establishing New Culture

"I establish a culture of faith, boldness, and sound mind in my sphere of influence. Fear has no place in our midst."

Steps to Maintain Freedom

1. **Daily Warfare Routine**
    - Morning declarations
    - Scripture meditation
    - Strategic prayer
    - Praise and worship

2. **Regular Spiritual Hygiene**
    - Check for fear's influence
    - Clean thought patterns
    - Guard heart boundaries
    - Maintain faith focus

3. **Community Support**
    - Build accountability
    - Share testimonies
    - Pray together
    - Support growth

A Leader's Prayer for the People

Father, I stand in the gap for those You've placed under my leadership. I break the power of fear over their lives. I declare freedom from every spirit that has partnered with fear. Release Your perfect love to cast out all fear. Establish Your peace, power, and sound mind in their lives.

Lord, teach them to war against fear. Show them how to use Your Word as a weapon. Train their hands for battle and their fingers for war against this spirit. Let them rise up in authority and walk in complete freedom from fear's influence.

In Jesus' name, Amen.

Remember: As leaders, our victory over fear isn't just personal – it's prophetic. It declares to every generation that fear's chains can be broken, its lessons can be unlearned, and its influence can be permanently overcome through strategic spiritual warfare and the power of God's Word.

Section 1: The Theology and Nature of Fear as a Spirit - Understanding Immani

The Mothership of Fear: Understanding Immani

The Etymology and Authority of Immani

The spirit of fear, known in its root form as Immani, operates as a principality level spirit - a mothership from which tributary spirits of fear emerge and operate. The name Immani carries within it the essence of:

- Terrorizing dominion
- Overwhelming dread
- Paralyzing horror
- Consuming anxiety
- Death-realm authority

This spirit's name reveals its operational mandate: to establish death's dominion over the thoughts, emotions, and decisions of humanity, particularly targeting those called to significant kingdom purpose.

The Council of Torment

Immani operates not in isolation but as the head of a tormenting council. This hierarchical structure includes:

1. **Primary Council Members**
    - Spirit of Terror (Sudden Fear)
    - Spirit of Dread (Ongoing Fear)
    - Spirit of Horror (Paralyzing Fear)

- Spirit of Anxiety (Consuming Fear)
- Spirit of Panic (Overwhelming Fear)

2. **Secondary Operators**
   - Spirits of Phobia
   - Spirits of Trauma
   - Spirits of Paranoia
   - Spirits of Obsession
   - Spirits of Compulsion

3. **Support Spirits**
   - Spirit of Mental Torment
   - Spirit of Emotional Instability
   - Spirit of Physical Manifestation
   - Spirit of Relational Disruption
   - Spirit of Spiritual Interference

The Operational Structure of Fear's Domain

1. The Throne of Death

Immani establishes its authority through death's throne:

1. **Death's Influence Over Thought**
   - Thoughts of suicide
   - Thoughts of failure
   - Thoughts of destruction
   - Thoughts of loss
   - Thoughts of doom

2. **Death's Domain Over Emotion**
   - Death of peace
   - Death of joy
   - Death of hope

- Death of love
- Death of trust

3. **Death's Rule Over Decisions**
   - Death of vision
   - Death of purpose
   - Death of relationships
   - Death of opportunities
   - Death of destiny

2. The Carnal Mind's Susceptibility

"For to be carnally minded is death" (Romans 8:6)

The carnal mind serves as fertile ground for Immani's operation:

1. **Points of Entry**
   - Unrenewed thinking
   - Worldly perspectives
   - Fleshly reactions
   - Natural reasoning
   - Human logic

2. **Areas of Influence**
   - Thought patterns
   - Belief systems
   - Value structures
   - Decision processes
   - Emotional responses

3. **Manifestation Zones**
   - Mental realm
   - Emotional realm
   - Physical realm

- Spiritual realm
- Relational realm

The Structure of Fear's Operation

1. The Root System

Immani establishes deep root systems through:

1. **Generational Lines**
   - Ancestral trauma
   - Family patterns
   - Inherited fears
   - Genetic memory
   - Bloodline curses

2. **Personal Experience**
   - Childhood trauma
   - Life events
   - Significant losses
   - Major failures
   - Overwhelming situations

3. **Environmental Factors**
   - Cultural influences
   - Societal pressures
   - Community trauma
   - Collective fear
   - Atmospheric principalities

2. The Fruit Production

From these roots, Immani produces specific fruits:

1. **Behavioral Fruits**
   - Avoidance patterns
   - Escape mechanisms
   - Control behaviors
   - Protection systems
   - Defense structures

2. **Emotional Fruits**
   - Chronic anxiety
   - Persistent worry
   - Constant dread
   - Ongoing terror
   - Perpetual panic

3. **Spiritual Fruits**
   - Faith paralysis
   - Prayer hesitation
   - Worship inhibition
   - Service restriction
   - Fellowship limitation

The Strategic Operations of Immani

1. Primary Tactical Approaches

Immani employs specific strategies:

1. **Mind Manipulation**
   - Thought distortion
   - Reality warping
   - Truth twisting
   - Perspective shifting
   - Memory corruption

2. **Emotional Warfare**
   - Feeling amplification
   - Mood destabilization
   - Emotional hijacking
   - Affective flooding
   - Sensory overwhelm

3. **Spiritual Interference**
   - Faith disruption
   - Hope destruction
   - Love contamination
   - Peace elimination
   - Joy suppression

2. Secondary Support Operations

Supporting tactics include:

1. **Physical Manifestations**
   - Body responses
   - Health impacts
   - Sleep disruption
   - Energy depletion
   - Systemic reactions

2. **Relational Disruption**
   - Connection severance
   - Trust destruction
   - Intimacy prevention
   - Community isolation
   - Partnership dissolution

3. **Destiny Interference**
   - Purpose delay
   - Vision distortion
   - Calling prevention
   - Gift suppression
   - Mandate interference

The Biblical Evidence of Immani's Operation

1. Old Testament Manifestations

1. **The Garden**
   - Fear's entry point
   - Hiding from God
   - Relationship disruption
   - Purpose deviation
   - Identity distortion

2. **Israel's Journey**
   - Wilderness fear
   - Giant fear
   - Future fear
   - Battle fear
   - Change fear

3. **Prophetic Encounters**
   - Elijah's flight
   - Jeremiah's hesitation
   - Isaiah's unworthiness
   - Moses' reluctance
   - David's moments

2. New Testament Revelations

1. **Jesus' Confrontations**
   - Storm fear
   - Death fear
   - Future fear
   - Persecution fear
   - Provision fear

2. **Apostolic Challenges**
   - Peter's denial
   - Thomas' doubt
   - Paul's thorn
   - John Mark's retreat
   - Timothy's timidity

Spiritual Warfare in Corporate America: Defeating Fear in Business and Organizational Structures

Biblical Precedents of Organizational Fear

1. Nehemiah's Construction Company

Nehemiah faced multiple manifestations of fear while rebuilding Jerusalem's walls:

1. **Operational Fear**
   - Workers afraid to build
   - Teams dividing their focus between work and defense
   - Productivity threatened by constant threat
   - Project timeline impacts
   - Resource allocation challenges

2. **Leadership Response**
   - "Don't be afraid of them. Remember the Lord, who is great and awesome" (Nehemiah 4:14)
   - Strategic positioning of guards
   - Maintaining work despite threats
   - Clear communication channels
   - Balanced resource management

2. Solomon's Kingdom Enterprise

Solomon's vast business operations provide insights into organizational structure:

1. **Scale of Operation**
   - International trade
   - Multiple revenue streams
   - Large workforce
   - Complex supply chains
   - Diverse partnerships

2. **Wisdom Principles**
   - "The fear of the Lord is the beginning of wisdom" (Proverbs 9:10)
   - Distinguished between godly and ungodly fear
   - Built systems on wisdom
   - Established clear protocols
   - Maintained divine perspective

Identifying Fear in Corporate Structures

3. **1. Cultural Indicators**
1. **Team Dynamics**
   - Excessive meetings for simple decisions

- Reluctance to share ideas
- Blame-shifting behaviors
- Silo mentality
- Information hoarding

2. **Communication Patterns**
   - Over-documentation for protection
   - Passive-aggressive exchanges
   - Limited upward communication
   - Defensive reporting
   - Minimal creative input

3. **Leadership Behaviors**
   - Micromanagement
   - Delayed decision-making
   - Risk aversion
   - Innovation resistance
   - Control addiction

2. Operational Symptoms

1. **Process Indicators**
   - Unnecessary bureaucracy
   - Excessive approvals required
   - Rigid adherence to outdated procedures
   - Resistance to change
   - Over-complication of simple tasks

2. **Performance Metrics**
   - Decreased productivity
   - Increased error rates
   - Lower innovation rates

- Reduced market share
- Declining profitability

3. **Resource Management**
   - Conservative budgeting
   - Underutilized assets
   - Minimal investment in growth
   - High cash reserves
   - Limited expansion

The Impact of Fear on Profitability

1. Direct Financial Effects

1. **Revenue Impact**
   - Missed market opportunities
   - Conservative pricing strategies
   - Limited market expansion
   - Reduced customer acquisition
   - Decreased sales activity

2. **Cost Implications**
   - Higher operational costs due to inefficiency
   - Increased compliance expenses
   - Excessive insurance coverage
   - Redundant systems
   - Over-staffing for security

3. **Investment Consequences**
   - Delayed capital investments
   - Missed growth opportunities
   - Underutilized resources
   - Limited R&D spending

- Restricted marketing budgets

2. Indirect Financial Effects

1. **Human Capital Costs**
   - Increased turnover
   - Higher training expenses
   - Lower productivity
   - Reduced innovation
   - Decreased engagement

2. **Market Position Impact**
   - Lost market share
   - Reduced competitive advantage
   - Diminished brand value
   - Weakened market presence
   - Limited market influence

Spiritual Warfare Strategies for Business

1. Corporate Prayer Protocols

1. **Strategic Prayer Points**
   - Declaration over company culture
   - Breaking fear's hold on decision-making
   - Releasing wisdom and innovation
   - Establishing divine protection
   - Activating kingdom prosperity

2. **Team Prayer Initiatives**
   - Department prayer coverage
   - Project-specific prayer
   - Crisis intervention prayer

- Strategic planning prayer
- Market breakthrough prayer

2. Prophetic Business Actions

1. **Faith-Based Initiatives**
   - Bold market moves
   - Innovation launches
   - Strategic expansions
   - Partnership development
   - Market leadership

2. **Kingdom Principles**
   - Integrity-based decisions
   - Value-driven operations
   - Purpose-aligned strategies
   - Faith-powered leadership
   - Spirit-led innovation

Breaking Fear's Corporate Strongholds

1. Leadership Actions

1. **Cultural Transformation**
   - Establish faith-based culture
   - Encourage calculated risks
   - Reward innovation
   - Promote open communication
   - Build trust-based systems

2. **Structural Changes**
   - Streamline decision processes
   - Remove unnecessary barriers

- Create empowerment structures
- Develop support systems
- Install feedback mechanisms

2. Spiritual Protocols

1. Corporate Deliverance

"In the name of Jesus Christ:
- We break the spirit of fear over this organization
- We cancel every assignment of Immani in our operations
- We destroy fear-based systems and structures
- We establish kingdom authority in our business
- We release divine wisdom and courage"

2. Maintaining Freedom
- Regular spiritual audits
- Cultural health checks
- Leadership alignment
- Team empowerment
- Kingdom accountability

Practical Application Steps

1. Assessment Phase

1. Cultural Audit
- Fear indicators checklist
- Team surveys
- Process analysis
- Decision pattern review
- Communication assessment

2. **Spiritual Mapping**
   - Identify spiritual strongholds
   - Map fear patterns
   - Locate entry points
   - Track manifestations
   - Document impacts

2. Implementation Phase

1. **Strategic Actions**
   - Define clear vision
   - Establish new protocols
   - Train leadership
   - Empower teams
   - Monitor progress

2. **Spiritual Initiatives**
   - Corporate prayer strategy
   - Leadership intercession
   - Team spiritual development
   - Kingdom culture building
   - Prophetic activation

Maintaining Corporate Freedom

1. Regular Assessment

1. **Performance Metrics**
   - Track key indicators
   - Monitor cultural health
   - Measure decision speed
   - Evaluate innovation rate
   - Assess market boldness

2. **Spiritual Health**
   - Prayer effectiveness
   - Faith atmosphere
   - Team courage
   - Leadership boldness
   - Kingdom alignment

2. **Continuous Development**

1. **Leadership Growth**
   - Courage development
   - Faith building
   - Wisdom acquisition
   - Strategic thinking
   - Spiritual authority

2. **Team Empowerment**
   - Skills development
   - Authority delegation
   - Decision making
   - Innovation encouragement
   - Risk management

Prayer for Corporate Liberation

Father, in the name of Jesus, we take authority over every spirit of fear operating in our organization. We break the power of Immani over our corporate structure, culture, and operations. We declare freedom in our decision-making, boldness in our market approach, and wisdom in our strategy.

We loose creativity, innovation, and kingdom prosperity. We bind fear, control, and limitation. We declare this organization a fear-free zone where Your Spirit rules, where wisdom flows, and where kingdom purposes are fulfilled.

Release supernatural strategies, divine connections, and marketplace favor. Let this business be a testimony of Your power and a channel of Your prosperity.

In Jesus' name, Amen.

Welcome To Part 2: Unmasking the Hidden Fears in Leadership

Listen.

I need to pause right here and acknowledge something – if Part 1 of this book hit you hard, if it exposed things you weren't ready to see, if it made you uncomfortable... good. That's exactly what it was supposed to do. Fear has a way of creating these dark, hidden spaces in our minds where truth can't penetrate. It's like setting up black curtains in our intellect, blocking out the light that could expose what's really holding us back from walking in the freedom God promised us as leaders.

Let me be real with you for a moment.

I know what it is to lead while fear is choking out your vision. I know what it is to love while fear is whispering "what if they leave?" I know what it is to lie in bed at night while fear plays horror movies in your mind about tomorrow. I know what it is to make business decisions with fear sitting at the board table.

But family, I also know what it is to do all these things in faith.

I know what it is to lead with bold vision. I know what it is to love without restraint. I know what it is to sleep in perfect peace. I know what it is to make decisions anchored in wisdom and confidence.

The journey from one reality to the other – that's what this second part of our book is about.

WHAT THE FEAR IS GOING ON

In these next chapters, we're going to deal with some specific fears that love to hide in the hearts of leaders, both in ministry and in the marketplace. We're going to pull back those curtains and let the light expose every hidden thing. We're going to name these fears, understand their operation, and most importantly, learn how to defeat them.

But before you turn this page and dive in, I need you to do something for me.

Take a breath.

Maybe even take a break.

Because what's coming next requires something from you that fear hates – honesty. Raw, uncomfortable, life-changing honesty with yourself about what's really going on inside. The kind of honesty that makes fear tremble because it knows its hiding places are about to be exposed.

Prepare your heart. Brace your spirit. Get ready to be uncomfortably honest with yourself.

Because the freedom waiting on the other side of that honesty? It's worth every uncomfortable moment.

It's worth every tear. Worth every confession. Worth every revelation.

I know, because I've walked this path. And now, I'm going to walk it with you.

Let's expose these hidden fears together. Let's break these chains together. Let's step into freedom together.

The light is about to shine in some dark places. Are you ready?

Let's go.

CHAPTER 6
CONFRONTING HIDDEN FEARS

Leadership positions often come with a myriad of responsibilities and challenges, requiring individuals to navigate complex situations with confidence and clarity. However, hidden fears can undermine a leader's effectiveness, hindering their decision-making abilities and impacting team dynamics. It is crucial for leaders to identify and address these fears to unlock their full potential and lead with authenticity. One common fear that holds back leaders is the fear of failure. This fear can stem from past experiences or a perfectionist mindset that sets unrealistic expectations. Leaders who are afraid of failure may avoid taking risks or making bold decisions, ultimately limiting their growth and the success of their team. By acknowledging this fear and reframing failure as a learning opportunity rather than a setback, leaders can cultivate resilience and innovation in their leadership approach. Another prevalent fear among leaders is the fear of vulnerability. In a competitive business environment, showing vulnerability can be perceived as a sign of weakness, leading some leaders to adopt a facade of invulnerability.

However, true leadership requires authenticity and emotional intelligence, which necessitate embracing vulnerability as a strength rather than a liability. By confronting this fear head-on and fostering open communication within their teams, leaders can build trust and foster meaningful connections that drive organizational success. Moreover, the fear of change is another significant obstacle that many leaders face. The rapidly evolving business landscape demands adaptability and agility from leaders, yet the uncertainty associated with change can trigger anxiety and resistance. Leaders who are able to confront this fear by cultivating a growth mindset and embracing innovation can position themselves as catalysts for transformation within their organizations. By recognizing these hidden fears, leaders can embark on a journey of self-discovery and empowerment that enables them to lead authentically, inspire others, and drive positive change within their organizations.

Hidden Yet Visible: The Fears You Think You're Hiding

Let me tell you something that might shake you up a bit.

Those fears you think you've hidden so well? The ones you've tucked away behind that powerful leadership persona? They're about as hidden as an elephant wearing a baseball cap. Your team sees them. Your organization feels them. Your ministry experiences them.

The Illusion of Hidden Fear

Listen, I've been there. Standing in front of my team, thinking I had everything locked down tight. My fears? Neatly packed away in boxes labeled "Handle Later" or "Not Important" or my personal favorite, "Nobody Needs to Know This." But here's the truth that humbled me – while I was busy hiding these fears, they were broadcasting themselves on every frequency my leadership touched.

Your fears speak through:
- The decisions you hesitate to make
- The conversations you avoid having
- The risks you refuse to take
- The trust you struggle to extend
- The control you can't seem to release

Your team doesn't need a prophetic anointing to see what you're afraid of. They just need to watch you lead for a week.

The Public Display of Private Fears

Let me break this down for you:

1. The Fear of Failure

You think you're hiding it through:
- Excessive micromanagement
- Over-preparation
- Perfectionist tendencies
- Decision paralysis

Your team sees it in:
- Their inability to take initiative
- The suffocating approval processes
- The culture of fear around mistakes
- The lack of innovation

2. The Fear of Inadequacy

You think you're hiding it through:
- Name-dropping
- Credential-stacking
- Achievement-hoarding
- Authority-flexing

Your team sees it in:
- Your need to be the smartest in the room
- Your resistance to their growth
- Your difficulty receiving feedback
- Your constant self-promotion

3. The Fear of Losing Control

You think you're hiding it through:

- Detailed protocols
- Excessive reporting
- Constant oversight
- Information hoarding

Your team sees it in:
- Their lack of empowerment
- The bottlenecked decisions
- The stifled creativity
- The absence of delegation

4. The Fear of Betrayal

You think you're hiding it through:
- Limited vulnerability
- Emotional distance
- Trust issues
- Relationship walls

Your team sees it in:
- The lack of authentic connection
- The surface-level relationships
- The difficulty in building team unity
- The absence of genuine collaboration

The Power of Vulnerable Leadership

Now, here's where it gets good. Here's where we flip the script on fear.

What if I told you that your fears, properly acknowledged and vulnerably shared, could become one of your greatest leadership assets?

Let me testify.

The day I stood before my team and admitted my fear of failure, was the day they started taking more risks. Why? Because they saw their leader being human enough to acknowledge struggle but faithful enough to push through it.

When I shared my journey with imposter syndrome, it created a culture where others could be honest about their own battles with adequacy. My vulnerability became their permission to be authentic.

The Transform-ational Power of Transparency

Here's what happens when you get honest about your fears:

1. **You Build Real Trust**
    - Authenticity breeds authenticity
    - Vulnerability creates connection
    - Honesty establishes credibility
    - Transparency generates trust

2. **You Create Safe Spaces**
    - For others to be honest
    - For genuine growth
    - For true collaboration
    - For innovative thinking

3. **You Model Growth**
    - Showing how to face fears
    - Demonstrating emotional intelligence
    - Exhibiting personal development
    - Inspiring intentional growth

4. **You Release Others**
    - From perfectionist pressure
    - From fear of failure
    - From imposter syndrome

- From performance anxiety

The Strategic Advantage of Acknowledged Fear

Let me be clear – I'm not talking about dumping all your fears on your team. This isn't about emotional vomit in the conference room. This is about strategic vulnerability that:

1. **Builds Strength**
    - Shows how to face challenges
    - Demonstrates resilience
    - Exhibits courage
    - Models growth

2. **Creates Connection**
    - Establishes relatability
    - Develops empathy
    - Fosters understanding
    - Builds community

3. **Empowers Others**
    - Gives permission to be human
    - Encourages authentic leadership
    - Promotes healthy risk-taking
    - Facilitates growth

A New Way Forward

Here's your invitation to a different kind of leadership:

1. **Acknowledge Your Fears**
    - To yourself first
    - To God consistently
    - To mentors regularly
    - To your team appropriately

2. **Share Your Journey**
   - Not just your struggles
   - But also your victories
   - Not just your fears
   - But also your faith

3. **Create Culture Change**
   - From hiding to healing
   - From pretense to authenticity
   - From fear to faith
   - From isolation to community

The Promise in Vulnerability

Remember this: Your vulnerability about fear isn't a leadership liability – it's a leadership asset. When handled with wisdom, it becomes:

- A bridge to genuine connection
- A catalyst for team growth
- A foundation for authentic culture
- A pathway to greater impact

Your team doesn't need you to be fearless. They need you to be faithful. Faithful enough to acknowledge your fears. Faithful enough to face them. Faithful enough to show others how to do the same.

Stop hiding what's already visible. Start leveraging your journey with fear to create something powerful in your organization. Because here's the truth – your greatest impact as a leader might not come from your strengths, but from your willingness to be honest about your struggles.

Let your fears become the fertile ground where authenticity grows and real leadership flourishes.

That's not a weakness. That's wisdom. That's not vulnerability. That's victory.

The Chameleon Spirit: Fear's Ability to Color Every Season

The Nature of the Chameleon Spirit

Let me tell you about one of fear's most dangerous characteristics – its chameleon nature. This ain't just about fear changing colors; this is about how fear becomes whatever it needs to become to survive in whatever environment you step into.

Think about a chameleon for a minute. It doesn't just change colors for fun. It shifts its appearance to blend perfectly with whatever surface it's on. Green leaf? Green chameleon. Brown branch? Brown chameleon. That's exactly how fear operates in your life.

The Manifestation Principle

Here's what you need to understand: Fear isn't just something that follows you – it's something that lives within you. And whatever lives within you will manifest wherever you go. It's a spiritual principle you can't escape:

- What's in you will come out of you
- What's in you will color your environment
- What's in you will shape your experience
- What's in you will influence your impact

The Chameleon's Shifting Colors

Let me break this down for you:

1. In Business

- Your internal fear of failure becomes excessive control
- Your fear of lack becomes unhealthy money decisions
- Your fear of competition becomes unethical practices
- Your fear of exposure becomes defensive leadership
- Your fear of inadequacy becomes micromanagement

2. In Relationships

- Your fear of abandonment becomes toxic attachment
- Your fear of vulnerability becomes emotional walls
- Your fear of betrayal becomes controlling behavior
- Your fear of intimacy becomes relational distance
- Your fear of commitment becomes perpetual sabotage

3. In Ministry

- Your fear of judgment becomes performance-based service
- Your fear of responsibility becomes limited impact
- Your fear of exposure becomes surface-level ministry
- Your fear of failure becomes safe preaching
- Your fear of man becomes compromised conviction

4. In Leadership

- Your fear of inadequacy becomes authoritarian leadership
- Your fear of loss becomes possessive management
- Your fear of failure becomes risk-averse decision making
- Your fear of criticism becomes defensive communication
- Your fear of success becomes self-sabotaging behaviors

The Transition Truth

Listen carefully: Every new level of transition becomes a new canvas for your internal fears to paint themselves upon. Your promotion isn't just a new position – it's a new surface for your chameleon fear to blend into.

That's why you see people:

- Get a new position but carry old problems
- Enter new relationships but repeat old patterns
- Start new ministries but manifest old limitations

- Launch new businesses but live out old fears

The Awakening of Dormant Fear

Understand this principle: Transition doesn't create new fears; it awakens dormant ones. Like a chameleon that's been sleeping on one branch, when you move to a new branch (transition), it doesn't become a new chameleon – it's the same chameleon adapting to a new environment.

Your undealt-with fears will:

- Adapt to new environments
- Adjust to new situations
- Align with new challenges
- Appear in new forms

Breaking the Chameleon Cycle

To break this cycle, you must:

1. Identify the Core Fear
- Not just its manifestations
- Not just its expressions
- Not just its symptoms
- But its root

2. Confront the Internal Reality
- Address what's within
- Deal with what's inside
- Face what's resident
- Confront what's inherent

3. Apply Radical Deliverance
- Not surface treatment

- Not behavior modification
- Not circumstantial change
- But root extraction

The Liberation Process

1. **Recognition**
   - Identify fear's patterns
   - Note its adaptations
   - Track its manifestations
   - Map its expressions

2. **Extraction**
   - Deal with root causes
   - Address core issues
   - Confront original wounds
   - Handle foundational matters

3. **Replacement**
   - Install faith principles
   - Establish truth foundations
   - Build confidence structures
   - Develop courage habits

The Warning Signs

Watch for these indicators that your chameleon fear is active:

1. **Pattern Recognition**
   - Same issues, different places
   - Same problems, new positions
   - Same struggles, new seasons
   - Same fears, fresh environments

2. **Transition Triggers**
    - Promotion anxiety
    - Relationship repetition
    - Ministry manifestations
    - Leadership limitations

The Freedom Declaration

It's time to declare:
- "Fear will not color my new season"
- "Fear will not shape my next level"
- "Fear will not determine my expression"
- "Fear will not define my transition"

The Transformation Truth

Remember this: The goal isn't to change fear's color – it's to remove the chameleon completely. Don't manage fear's manifestations; eliminate its residence.

Because here's the liberating truth: When fear no longer lives within you, it can't manifest around you. When you're free internally, you're free to transition externally without fear painting its colors in your new season.

You're not called to adapt your fear. You're called to evict it. You're not called to manage its manifestations. You're called to eliminate its residence.

Deal with what's within, and what's around you will transform accordingly. That's not just freedom – that's transformation.

CHAPTER 7
FEAR OF THE UNKNOWN

> *"Yet there shall be a space between you and it, about two thousand cubits by measure. Do not come near it, that you may know the way by which you must go, for you have not passed this way before."*
> *– Joshua 3:4 (NKJV)*

The human psyche craves control, a deep-seated desire to feel a sense of mastery over our environment and our lives. This need for control is woven into our very being, a survival instinct that has served us well throughout history. In a world where uncertainty could mean the difference between life and death, seeking control allowed our ancestors to navigate the dangers of the unknown. This innate need for control has its benefits, providing a sense of stability and order in a chaotic world. It allows us to plan, to predict, and to feel a sense of agency over our actions. We create routines, build schedules, and set goals, all in an effort to impose structure and predictability on the seemingly random nature of life.

But what happens when this need for control becomes excessive? When we clutch onto the reins of our lives too tightly, fearing the very thought of relinquishing control? This is where the illusion of control takes root, a dangerous trap that can hinder growth, stifle creativity, and ultimately lead to a life lived in a state of constant anxiety.

In the realm of leadership, the illusion of control can have particularly detrimental effects. Leaders, often burdened with the responsibility of making decisions that impact the lives of others, can become paralyzed by the fear of the unknown. The constant pressure to maintain order and achieve desired outcomes can lead to a relentless pursuit of control, leaving little room for flexibility, adaptability, and innovation.

Imagine a CEO, driven by a deep-seated fear of failure, clinging tightly to every decision, micromanaging every detail, and shunning any suggestion that deviates from their carefully crafted plan. This leader, despite their good intentions, becomes a prisoner of their own anxieties, unable to see the potential benefits of embracing uncertainty and allowing their team to take risks and explore uncharted territory. The fear of losing control leads to stagnation, stifling the creativity and innovation that are essential for an organization to thrive in a rapidly changing world.

The need for control can also manifest as a resistance to change, a fear of stepping outside of the comfort zone of familiar routines and predictable outcomes. This fear can hold back both individuals and organizations from embracing opportunities for growth and development. We become so fixated on maintaining the status quo, fearing the unknown consequences of venturing into new territory, that we miss out on the potential for transformative breakthroughs and radical innovation.

The illusion of control can also lead to a focus on short-term gains at the expense of long-term sustainability. We become obsessed with immediate results, neglecting the importance of investing in long-term strategies and fostering a culture of adaptability. In a world where disruptions and unforeseen events are becoming increasingly commonplace, this short-sighted approach can lead to a lack of resilience and a failure to adapt to changing circumstances.

The pursuit of control can also have a corrosive effect on our relationships. We become so focused on maintaining order and asserting our authority that we fail to cultivate the trust and open communication that are essential for strong relationships. The fear of losing control can lead to a lack of empathy and a willingness to listen to others' perspectives, hindering collaboration and creating a culture of fear and mistrust.

But the illusion of control is just that, an illusion. The truth is that life is inherently uncertain, filled with unpredictable events and unexpected turns. The sooner we embrace this truth, the sooner we can free ourselves from the shackles of constant control and start to live a life filled with more freedom, flexibility, and resilience.

This is where the importance of confronting the fear of the unknown comes into play. This is not about surrendering to chaos or abandoning all sense of order. Instead, it is about learning to navigate uncertainty with a sense of confidence and adaptability. It is about recognizing that control is an illusion and embracing the power of letting go.

We need to shift our mindset from one of control to one of influence. Instead of trying to dictate every detail of our lives, we need to focus on fostering a culture of trust, empowerment, and adaptability. This means creating an environment where team members feel comfortable taking risks, embracing ambiguity, and learning from their mistakes.

It means creating a culture of continuous learning, where individuals are encouraged to develop their skills, expand their horizons, and be open to new ideas. It means fostering a sense of psychological safety, where team members feel comfortable sharing their ideas and concerns without fear of judgment or reprisal. The pursuit of control can be a seductive trap, promising a false sense of security and stability. But the truth is that true strength lies not in controlling every detail of our lives, but in embracing the unknown with courage and resilience. It is about letting go of the illusion of control and trusting in our ability to adapt, learn, and grow. This journey begins with a willingness to confront our fear of the unknown, to step outside of our comfort zones, and to embrace the challenges and opportunities that come with living in a world of constant change. It is about learning to dance with uncertainty, not fight against it, and discovering the hidden strengths and resilience that lie within us all.

WHAT THE FEAR IS GOING ON

When New Territory Meets Terror: A Leader's Battle with the Unknown

The Weight of Not Knowing

Let me talk to you for a minute about that heavy feeling that sits in your stomach when God calls you to lead people somewhere you've never been yourself. That moment when everyone's looking at you for answers, and all you've got is a promise and a direction.

Joshua knew this feeling. Standing at the edge of the Jordan, he wasn't just facing a river – he was facing every leader's greatest challenge: the unknown. After Moses, a man who spoke to God face to face, here stands Joshua, carrying not just the mandate but the expectations of an entire nation.

The Terror of Leadership Expectations

Let's be real about what creates terror in new territory:

1. The Pressure of Position

- Everyone expects you to have the answers
- Your team looks to you for certainty
- Your followers need your confidence
- Your critics wait for your failure

2. The Weight of Responsibility

- Lives depend on your decisions
- Families follow your direction
- Resources ride on your choices
- Destinies align with your obedience

3. The Burden of Legacy

- Following a great leader (Moses)
- Maintaining established standards

- Meeting historical expectations
- Creating future foundations

The Difference Between Territory and Terror

Now, watch this revelation:

New Territory is:
- God's invitation to expansion
- Heaven's opportunity for growth
- Divine platform for miracle
- Holy ground for testimony

Terror is:
- Enemy's distortion of opportunity
- Hell's corruption of challenge
- Demonic twisting of transition
- Spiritual poisoning of progress

Joshua's Victory Over Territory Terror

Let's examine how Joshua conquered the fear of the unknown:

1. He Focused on God's Presence, Not Personal Performance

"As I was with Moses, so I will be with you." (Joshua 1:5)
- Not about his capability
- But about God's faithfulness
- Not about his experience
- But about divine expertise

2. He Embraced the New Without Rejecting the Known
- Honored Moses's legacy
- Built on established foundation

- Applied timeless principles
- Created fresh applications

3. He Led from Revelation, Not Information

"When you see the ark of the covenant... follow it." (Joshua 3:3)
- Followed divine signals
- Watched for God's movement
- Waited for holy timing
- Moved by spiritual insight

The Pressure of Pioneering

Let me break down what makes new territory feel like terror:

1. **The Absence of Precedent**
   - No footprints to follow
   - No markers to guide
   - No examples to study
   - No patterns to copy

2. **The Weight of First**
   - First to face certain challenges
   - First to make certain decisions
   - First to cross certain boundaries
   - First to establish certain patterns

3. **The Cost of Mistake**
   - Impact on followers
   - Effect on future
   - Influence on legacy
   - Consequence on destiny

Breaking the Terror of Territory

Here's how to handle new territory without terror:

1. Change Your Perspective
- Unknown to God is not unknown
- Unfamiliar to you is not unfamiliar to Him
- Unprecedented to man is not unprecedented to Heaven
- Uncharted by others is not uncharted by the Spirit

2. Adjust Your Position

Instead of:
- "I don't know what to do" Say: "I know who to follow"

Instead of:
- "I've never been here before" Say: "But God has already been here"

Instead of:
- "I can't see the way" Say: "The Way sees me"

3. Modify Your Process
- From figuring it out to finding Him out
- From knowing the path to knowing the Guide
- From having answers to having access
- From managing details to maintaining devotion

The Power of Holy Uncertainty

Here's a revelation that will free you: Not knowing is not the same as not leading.

In fact, sometimes the most powerful leadership happens when:
- You're honest about not knowing
- You're authentic about seeking

- You're transparent about learning
- You're humble about following

Leading Through the Unknown

Practical steps for territory without terror:

1. Embrace the Learning Position
- Be a student of the journey
- Stay hungry for guidance
- Remain open to instruction
- Keep humble in process

2. Maintain Clear Communication
- Share the vision clearly
- Update the progress honestly
- Admit the challenges openly
- Celebrate the victories regularly

3. Build Trust Through Transparency
- Be authentic about not knowing
- Be clear about seeking God
- Be honest about the process
- Be consistent in character

The Promise in Unknown Territory

Remember these truths:

1. **New Territory Is**
   - God's vote of confidence
   - Heaven's trust in your leadership
   - Divine preparation completing
   - Spiritual promotion manifesting

2. **The Unknown Is**
   - Not your enemy
   - But your classroom
   - Not your terror
   - But your trainer

A Leader's Declaration Over Unknown Territory

Declare this:

"I may not know the way, But I know the Way Maker.

I may not have been here before, But I know Who holds here.

I may not see the end, But I know Who sees me.

I may not have the answers, But I know Who answers me.

I choose to:
- Walk in territory without terror
- Lead in uncertainty with understanding
- Guide with questions but without fear
- Direct through process but not panic"

The Freedom of Leading Forward

In closing, remember: The pressure to know everything is not from God. The expectation to never question is not from Heaven. The demand to always be certain is not from the Spirit.

True leadership is not about:
- Having every answer
- Knowing every step
- Seeing every end
- Understanding every detail

It's about:

- Knowing Who to trust
- Following His lead
- Hearing His voice
- Obeying His word

You don't have to fear what you don't know when you know Who holds what you don't know.

That's not just a leadership principle. That's leadership freedom.

Here are some ways we can embrace uncertainty and unlock its creative potential:

1. Cultivate a Growth Mindset:

The first step in embracing uncertainty is to cultivate a growth mindset, a belief that our abilities are not fixed but can be developed through effort and learning. Those with a growth mindset see challenges as opportunities for growth, not as threats to their competence. They are open to feedback, willing to experiment, and embrace the unknown as a chance to learn and expand their abilities.

2. Embrace Experimentation:

In a world that often prioritizes certainty, the power of experimentation is often overlooked. But embracing experimentation is essential for innovation. It's about being comfortable with the unknown, testing new ideas, and learning from failures. By encouraging a culture of experimentation, leaders empower their teams to take risks, explore new possibilities, and ultimately, drive innovation.

3. Encourage Flexible Thinking:

Uncertainty often requires us to adapt our thinking. Rigid approaches and inflexible mindsets can hinder our ability to navigate changing circumstances. Leaders must encourage flexible thinking, the ability to adjust plans and strategies as new information emerges. By fostering a culture of open communication and collaborative problem-solving, leaders can empower their teams to think creatively and find innovative solutions to unexpected challenges.

4. Foster a Culture of Innovation:

Innovation thrives in an environment that embraces uncertainty. Leaders must create a culture where taking risks, experimenting, and learning from failures are valued. This means fostering a sense of psychological safety, where team members feel comfortable sharing ideas, challenging assumptions, and taking risks without fear of judgment or retribution.

5. Seek Out Diverse Perspectives:

When faced with uncertainty, it's tempting to retreat into familiar patterns and rely on our own experiences. However, to navigate ambiguity effectively, we need to seek out diverse perspectives. By engaging with individuals with different backgrounds, experiences, and ways of thinking, we broaden our understanding, challenge our assumptions, and gain new insights that can lead to innovative solutions.

6. Practice Active Listening:

Active listening is a powerful tool for navigating uncertainty. It's about truly understanding the perspectives and concerns of others. By listening attentively, asking clarifying questions, and seeking to understand the "why" behind people's views, leaders can gain valuable insights and make informed decisions.

7. Embrace the Power of "And":

When faced with uncertainty, our minds often resort to binary thinking: "either this or that." We tend to focus on what we know and reject what we don't. But in the realm of uncertainty, the power of "and" is crucial. It allows us to embrace multiple possibilities, consider different perspectives, and create solutions that are more comprehensive and innovative.

8. Learn from Failure:

Failure is an inevitable part of the journey, especially when embracing uncertainty. But instead of viewing failure as a setback, embrace it as a valuable learning experience. By conducting post-mortems, analyzing what went wrong, and adapting our strategies, we can transform failures into opportunities for growth and innovation.

Embracing uncertainty is not about eliminating risk or seeking comfort in the familiar. It's about recognizing that uncertainty is a catalyst for creativity and innovation. By cultivating a growth mindset, embracing experimentation, fostering flexible thinking, and seeking out diverse perspectives, leaders can transform their fear of the unknown into a source of strength, resilience, and innovation.

The journey of leadership, like life itself, is filled with uncertainties. It's in the heart of this ambiguity that we discover the power of creativity, the resilience of our spirit, and the potential for groundbreaking innovations.

Imagine a world where the future is a blank canvas, each day presenting a new set of possibilities, a symphony of opportunities waiting to be orchestrated. This is the realm of uncertainty, a terrain that can evoke both trepidation and exhilaration. While some might find comfort in the predictability of routine, it's within the embrace of the unknown that true growth and innovation take root.

The fear of the unknown is a primal instinct, a protective mechanism that has served our species well throughout history. However, in the modern world, where change is the only constant, this fear can become a barrier to progress, hindering our ability to adapt and thrive in a rapidly evolving landscape.

To navigate this uncertain world with confidence, we must cultivate adaptability as a core competency. This is not about simply rolling with the punches; it's about actively shaping our responses to the unforeseen, transforming challenges into opportunities for growth and learning.

Active Listening: The Key to Understanding Change

Adaptability begins with the ability to perceive change, not just as a threat, but as a signal of opportunity. Active listening is the cornerstone of this perception. It's more than simply hearing words; it's about engaging with the nuances of communication, the subtle cues that reveal underlying motivations and emotions.

Think of it as a mental compass, guiding us through the shifting currents of information. When we listen actively, we open ourselves to new perspectives, challenging our own assumptions and developing a richer understanding of the landscape around us.

For leaders, active listening is a powerful tool for fostering trust and collaboration. By genuinely seeking to understand the perspectives of their team members, leaders can create a sense of shared purpose and a collaborative environment where ideas can flourish.

Flexible Thinking: Embracing the Art of the Pivot

Adaptability demands a flexible mindset, the ability to adjust plans and strategies based on changing circumstances. This is not about abandoning our goals, but rather about recognizing that the path to achieving them may not always be linear.

Imagine yourself standing at the foot of a mountain, your destination the summit. A rigid plan might dictate a specific route, but along the way, unforeseen obstacles might arise: raging rivers, treacherous cliffs, or impassable snowdrifts. A flexible thinker, like a seasoned mountaineer, is prepared to adjust their route, seeking alternative paths and leveraging unexpected opportunities.

This mindset requires embracing ambiguity, allowing for a degree of uncertainty in our plans. It's about being comfortable with the unknown, recognizing that sometimes, the most creative solutions arise from the unexpected detours.

Adjusting Plans with Confidence: The Power of Iteration

Adaptability is not just about reacting to change; it's about proactively anticipating it and incorporating it into our decision-making. We can't predict the future, but we can build the capacity to respond to it effectively.

Think of it as a game of chess, where each move is a calculated response to the opponent's actions. A successful chess player anticipates their opponent's moves, adjusts their strategy accordingly, and adapts to the ever-changing dynamics of the game.

In a business context, this means developing a culture of iteration, a willingness to test, learn, and adjust based on the feedback we receive. It's about recognizing that failure is not the end, but rather a stepping stone on the path to success.

When God Calls You to Leave What You Love: My Journey into the Unknown

Let me take you back to one of the scariest moments of my life – when God called me to leave a place I absolutely loved.

I wasn't running from something bad. I wasn't escaping abuse or fleeing dysfunction. This was harder. This was good. This was leaving love.

Let me paint the picture for you.

I had grown up in this church. My fingerprints were all over the ministry – from playing in the music department to teaching Sunday school, from youth ministry to various leadership roles. This wasn't just my church; this was my family. These weren't just my leaders; these were my spiritual parents. This wasn't just my ministry; this was my life.

Then one day, in the midst of all this good, all this familiar, all this comfort – God spoke.

"It's time to go."

Y'all, can I be real with you? I fought that word for two whole years. Two years of wrestling. Two years of questioning. Two years of that uncomfortable space between knowing what God said and being willing to do it.

Because here's what nobody tells you about the unknown – it's not just about what you're going toward; it's about what you're leaving behind.

The Weight of Transition

I remember sitting in my room, trying to imagine what life would look like without:

- My regular seat in the sanctuary
- My position in ministry
- My familiar relationships
- My comfortable routines
- My spiritual family

The unknown wasn't just scary – it was physically heavy. It sat in my chest like a weight, pressed on my mind like a vice, wrapped around my heart like a chain.

The Cost of Obedience

When I finally gathered the courage to tell my leaders, I got some pushback. That little resistance almost made me retreat. "Maybe I heard God wrong," I thought. "Maybe this discomfort is a sign."

But God's voice remained clear: "It's time."

What followed was one of the most challenging seasons of my life. The warfare was intense:

- People called me rebellious
- Some labeled me disobedient
- Others questioned my character

- My own mother was pulled into it

The peak of the pain came when my mother was brought before the congregation with accusations that I was practicing witchcraft with her clothing. In that moment, the unknown didn't just feel scary – it felt like it was destroying everything I held dear.

The Temptation to Retreat

Can I be honest? There were moments when I thought: "If I had known it would cost this much…" "If I had known it would hurt this bad…" "If I had known it would look like this…"

The familiar bondage started looking better than the painful freedom. The known limitations started feeling safer than the uncertain liberty.

The Faithfulness in the Fire

But here's where the story shifts.

God started proving Himself not just faithful to me, but faithful to the word He gave me. What looked like chaos was actually clearing. What felt like destruction was actually direction. What seemed like an end was actually an entrance.

Today, I pastor multiple churches. The unknown territory God called me into has become fertile ground for ministry I couldn't have imagined. But let me be clear – this testimony isn't about leaving being right and staying being wrong. This isn't about my old church being bad and my new season being good.

This is about something deeper:

- The price of obedience
- The cost of the unknown
- The warfare of transition
- The reward of trust

The Beauty of Both/And

Here's what makes this story even more beautiful – I still love my former leaders. We still fellowship. I still honor what they poured into me. God's new thing didn't require me to despise the old thing. My obedience didn't demand my hatred of what I left.

They were good then. They are good now. God was good then. God is good now.

A Word for Those Facing the Unknown

So let me encourage you, leader. If you're standing at the edge of your own unknown:

1. **It's Okay to Love What You're Leaving**
   - Honor your past
   - Cherish your memories
   - Celebrate your growth
   - Thank your makers

2. **It's Okay to Fear What's Ahead**
   - Feel your emotions
   - Process your concerns
   - Voice your anxieties
   - Express your doubts

3. **It's Okay to Take Time**
   - Don't rush the process
   - Honor the journey
   - Respect the transition
   - Allow the preparation

But remember this:

The unknown will often call you before it shows you what it holds for you. The reward rarely precedes the obedience. The clarity seldom comes before the commitment.

Sometimes you have to:
- Step out to see
- Move to know
- Obey to understand
- Trust to triumph

The Promise in the Process

Today, I can tell you:
- The pain was worth it
- The cost was worth it
- The warfare was worth it
- The unknown was worth it

Not because everything turned out perfect, but because obedience always leads to purpose. Not because the transition was easy, but because God proved faithful.

So if you're facing your own unknown right now, if God's calling you to leave what you love, remember my story. Remember that:

- The warfare doesn't negate the word
- The pain doesn't void the promise
- The cost doesn't cancel the calling
- The unknown doesn't undo the anointing

Step out. Trust Him. Move forward. Embrace the unknown.

Because on the other side of your costly obedience is a testimony waiting to be told.

CHAPTER 8
FEAR OF REJECTION

> *"And Samuel said unto Jesse, 'Are here all thy children?' And he said, 'There remaineth yet the youngest, and, behold, he keepeth the sheep.' And Samuel said unto Jesse, 'Send and fetch him: for we will not sit down till he come hither.'"*
> *- 1 Samuel 16:11 (KJV)*

The fear of negative feedback can be a powerful and insidious force that hinders our personal and professional growth. It's a common human experience to crave validation and approval, and the thought of receiving criticism can feel like a personal attack, threatening our sense of worth and competence. We might avoid situations where feedback is likely, such as asking for constructive critiques, seeking mentors, or even participating in performance reviews. This avoidance strategy, however, can be incredibly detrimental.

Imagine a young entrepreneur who has poured their heart and soul into building a new business. They've worked tirelessly, sacrificing sleep and personal time to bring their vision to life. Now, they're finally ready to launch their product, and they're excited to receive feedback from potential customers. However, they are also terrified. What if people don't like it? What if they criticize their ideas? What if they find flaws that they haven't even considered?

This fear can be paralyzing, leading to inaction and missed opportunities. The entrepreneur might delay their launch, fearing the judgment of others. They might hesitate to share their ideas with potential investors, fearing rejection. They might avoid seeking feedback from mentors, fearing they might be criticized for their lack of experience. This cycle of avoidance can be incredibly detrimental, preventing the entrepreneur from growing, learning, and ultimately achieving their goals.

The truth is, feedback, whether positive or negative, is an invaluable gift. It's an opportunity to learn, grow, and improve. Negative feedback, in particular, can be incredibly insightful, providing us with a window into areas where we can enhance our performance. It's like a mirror, reflecting back to us the areas where we need to make adjustments and improve.

Consider the scenario of a seasoned executive presenting a strategic plan to their board of directors. They've spent weeks meticulously crafting the plan, pouring over data, and anticipating every potential objection. However, during the presentation, a board member raises a critical question, highlighting a potential flaw in the plan. The executive, overwhelmed by the fear of being judged, might become defensive, dismissing the feedback and clinging to their original strategy. They might even miss the opportunity to learn from the board member's insights, potentially jeopardizing the entire project.

In this scenario, the fear of negative feedback has clouded the executive's judgment, preventing them from seeing the value in the board member's critique. It's crucial to remember that feedback, even when it's challenging, is not personal. It's an opportunity to learn and grow, to refine our ideas, and to become better leaders.

Instead of becoming defensive, the executive could have acknowledged the board member's perspective, thanked them for their feedback, and engaged in a constructive dialogue. This open approach would have allowed the executive to learn from the feedback, revise their plan, and ultimately create a stronger and more effective strategy.

From Family Rejection to Global Influence: David's Path Through Opposition

The First Battlefield: Warfare in the House

Let's talk about that moment when David's own family didn't even consider him worthy to be present for his destiny.

Think about it:

- His father didn't call him in from the field
- His brothers didn't mention his existence
- His family proceeded without him
- His place at the table was empty

But watch this revelation: The first rejection a leader faces is often in their own house. Why? Because rejection at home builds the muscle you'll need for rejection in ministry.

The Hidden Training in Home Rejection

1. **Identity Formation**
    - Learning who you are when family doesn't see you
    - Understanding your worth isn't in recognition
    - Developing confidence without validation
    - Building strength in solitude

2. **Character Development**
    - Faithfulness in forgotten places
    - Excellence when no one's watching
    - Integrity in isolation
    - Purpose in obscurity

The Second Battlefield: Warfare Among the Sheep

Now, let's get into something deep. After David conquered home rejection, he faced wilderness rejection. But here's where it gets good:

The Lion Principle

Watch this revelation about the lion:

- The lion was king of the jungle
- When David defeated the lion, he defeated a kingdom
- Every other animal recognized this victory
- No other beast challenged what the lion couldn't defeat

Here's the principle: When you overcome the highest form of opposition in any realm, lesser opposition recognizes your authority.

The Strategic Value of Opposition

1. **Building Spiritual Authority**
   - Victory over the lion established dominion
   - Defeat of the bear confirmed authority
   - Lesser predators acknowledged the victory
   - Authority was established through conflict

2. **Developing Battle Strategy**
   - Learning warfare principles
   - Understanding enemy tactics
   - Developing victory patterns
   - Building battle confidence

The Third Battlefield: Warfare in the Kingdom

Then we see David at the battlefield with Goliath. Watch how rejection manifested:

- His brothers questioned his motives
- Saul doubted his ability
- The army dismissed his courage
- The enemy despised his youth

But here's the revelation: By this time, rejection had become David's gateway to opportunity.

The Progression of Rejection

1. **Family Rejection**
   - Built internal strength
   - Developed personal faith
   - Established private victory
   - Created emotional resilience

2. **Wilderness Rejection**
   - Proved his authority
   - Demonstrated his capacity
   - Confirmed his calling
   - Established his pattern

3. **Kingdom Rejection**
   - Positioned for public victory
   - Prepared for global impact
   - Platformed his anointing
   - Promoted his purpose

The Strategy of Heaven in Rejection

Understand this pattern:

1. **Local Rejection Creates Global Platform**
   - Family didn't want him at the anointing
   - Now nations would hear his story
   - Brothers didn't want him at the battle
   - Now generations would study his victory

2. **Private Rejection Prepares for Public Promotion**
   - Rejected in the house, respected in the kingdom

- Forgotten in the field, famous in the nation
- Dismissed by family, celebrated by multitudes
- Overlooked at home, honored abroad

The Leadership Principle

Here's what every leader needs to understand:

1. **Rejection is Not Your Enemy**
   - It's your trainer
   - It's your qualifier
   - It's your promoter
   - It's your platform

2. **Opposition is Not Your Obstacle**
   - It's your opportunity
   - It's your proof
   - It's your preparation
   - It's your pathway

The Process of Rejection to Reception

Watch the progression:

1. **House Rejection**
   - Develops character
   - Builds identity
   - Strengthens resolve
   - Deepens faith

2. **Field Victory**
   - Establishes authority
   - Proves capacity
   - Demonstrates ability

- Confirms calling

3. **Kingdom Impact**
   - Global influence
   - Generational impact
   - Historic significance
   - Divine purpose

A Word to Rejected Leaders

Understand this:
- Your family's rejection is forming your character
- Your local dismissal is developing your strength
- Your current opposition is creating your testimony
- Your present battle is building your legacy

Don't fight rejection – follow it:
- It's leading you to purpose
- It's guiding you to destiny
- It's preparing you for prominence
- It's positioning you for impact

The Promise in Rejection

Remember:
- David wasn't rejected from his destiny
- He was rejected into it
- He wasn't rejected from his purpose
- He was rejected toward it

Your rejection is not a roadblock; it's a gateway:
- From local to global
- From private to public
- From obscurity to influence

- From preparation to purpose

Let every rejection be a reminder: God doesn't just work despite rejection; He works through it. He doesn't just help you survive rejection; He uses it to stage your promotion.

That rejection you're facing? It's not your enemy. It's your elevator. It's not your destroyer. It's your developer.

Welcome to the pathway of promotion through rejection. This isn't your warfare. This is your gateway.

So, I have to pause and give you more insight on the lion principle to help open your eyes...

The Lion Principle: Understanding Your Authority

The Revelation of the Lion

Let me break something down for you that's going to shift how you see warfare. When David faced that lion in the wilderness, he wasn't just fighting a predator – he was engaging a principality. This wasn't just about protecting sheep; this was about establishing divine order in a territory.

The Anatomy of Lion Authority

In the natural realm, the lion represents:
- Supreme dominion
- Unchallenged authority
- Territorial rulership
- Kingdom governance

But watch this in the spirit:

When David confronted the lion, he was facing:
- The highest order of opposition
- The supreme authority in that realm

- The governing spirit of that territory
- The prince of that domain

The Kingdom Hierarchy Principle

Here's where it gets deep:

1. **The Lion's Position**
   - King of beasts
   - Ruler of territory
   - Master of domain
   - Supreme predator

2. **The Lion's Authority**
   - Other beasts submit
   - Lesser predators yield
   - Territory acknowledges
   - Domain recognizes

The Prophetic Revelation

Now watch this:

When David defeated the lion, he wasn't just winning a fight – he was:
- Dethroning a prince
- Displacing an authority
- Disrupting a hierarchy
- Dismantling a kingdom system

The Transfer of Authority

1. **What Happened in the Spirit**
   - Authority was transferred
   - Dominion was shifted

- Rulership was altered
- Kingdom was conquered

2. **What Changed in the Territory**
   - Every lesser beast recognized new authority
   - Every smaller predator acknowledged new ruler
   - Every opposing force submitted to new order
   - Every challenger recognized new dominion

The Spiritual Technology

Understand this principle:

1. **Supreme Victory Creates Territorial Authority**
   - Defeat the highest, influence the rest
   - Conquer the greatest, command the least
   - Overcome the strongest, rule the weakest
   - Master the mightiest, govern the smallest

2. **One Victory Establishes Multiple Authorities**
   - What you defeat no longer has right to defeat you
   - What you overcome cannot overcome you
   - What you conquer cannot conquer you
   - What you master cannot master you

The Application in Warfare

This principle operates in every realm:

1. **In Personal Warfare**
   - Defeat your greatest fear, lesser fears bow
   - Overcome your biggest giant, smaller ones fall
   - Conquer your main enemy, lesser ones flee
   - Master your primary battle, lesser ones submit

2. **In Ministry Warfare**
    - Defeat religious spirit, religious operations bow
    - Overcome major opposition, minor ones yield
    - Conquer primary resistance, secondary ones submit
    - Master main hindrance, lesser ones dissolve

3. **In Marketplace Warfare**
    - Defeat market leader, market acknowledges
    - Overcome industry giant, industry recognizes
    - Conquer main competitor, others respect
    - Master major challenge, minor ones bow

The Strategic Implementation

How to apply the Lion Principle:

1. **Identify Your Lion**
    - What's the highest opposition?
    - Who's the supreme challenger?
    - Where's the main resistance?
    - What's the primary battle?

2. **Engage with Understanding**
    - You're not just fighting an enemy
    - You're establishing authority
    - You're not just winning a battle
    - You're claiming territory

3. **Execute with Purpose**
    - Fight for transfer of authority
    - Battle for territorial rights
    - Contend for kingdom rulership
    - Wage war for domain influence

The Prophetic Pattern

Watch how this played out in David's life:

1. **The Lion Victory**
   - Established wilderness authority
   - Proved supernatural backing
   - Demonstrated divine support
   - Confirmed kingdom calling

2. **The Bear Confirmation**
   - Validated lion victory
   - Confirmed established authority
   - Reinforced divine pattern
   - Strengthened territorial claim

3. **The Goliath Manifestation**
   - Public display of private victory
   - National stage for wilderness authority
   - Global platform for local conquest
   - Kingdom demonstration of secret victories

The Current Application

For today's leaders:

1. **In Ministry**
   - Defeat main spiritual opposition
   - Territory will recognize authority
   - Realm will acknowledge anointing
   - Domain will submit to grace

2. **In Business**
   - Overcome primary market challenge
   - Industry will notice presence

- Field will respect position
- Sector will honor influence

3. **In Leadership**
    - Conquer major leadership challenge
    - Organization will follow vision
    - Team will trust direction
    - People will honor authority

The Warfare Warning

Remember:

1. **Don't Fight Lesser Battles**
    - Focus on supreme opposition
    - Target highest resistance
    - Engage primary enemy
    - Confront main adversary

2. **Don't Waste Energy**
    - Lesser victories don't transfer up
    - Small wins don't establish authority
    - Minor battles don't claim territory
    - Partial victories don't secure domain

The Promise in the Principle

Understand this:

- When you truly defeat the lion
- Everything under the lion's authority
- Must submit to your new authority
- Must recognize your victory
- Must acknowledge your position

Your lion battle isn't just about survival It's about supreme victory It's not just about winning It's about establishing

Therefore:

- Face your lion with understanding
- Fight your battle with purpose
- Finish your warfare with authority
- Fulfill your calling with power

Because when you defeat your lion:

- Territory transfers
- Authority shifts
- Domain submits
- Kingdom recognizes

This is more than principle This is kingdom technology This is warfare strategy This is victory protocol

Your lion isn't your destruction It's your door to domain authority It's not your defeat It's your pathway to supreme victory

Beyond the Wildlife: Conquering the Lion of Sexual Trauma

Let me share something deeply personal with you. When we talk about lions in our lives, some of us have had to face predators that attacked us before we even knew how to fight back.

The Seven-Year Mark

At seven years old, I encountered a predator that would try to define my entire life's jungle. Molestation isn't just an event - it's a lion that continues to hunt in your mind long after the physical attack is over. This lion didn't just wound my body; it tried to claim territory in my destiny.

The Battle of Two Natures

Here's where it gets real. After the molestation, I found myself in a war:

- My body pulling one way
- My mind fighting another
- My spirit knowing what's right
- My soul wrestling with what was done to me

I was dealing with what I call "the wildlife of perversion" - all these different manifestations of that original trauma:

- Confused attractions
- Sexual identity battles
- Relationship fears
- Intimacy struggles

Understanding the Jungle

But watch this revelation: In my journey to healing, I discovered something crucial about spiritual warfare. Many of us are out here fighting what I call "jungle wildlife":

- Random sexual thoughts
- Occasional temptations
- Periodic struggles
- Situational battles

But we never confront the lion - that main stronghold, that principality that keeps all other predators in place.

The Real Lion

For me, the lion wasn't just the sexual confusion - it was the deep-rooted perversion that the molestation had planted. This was the king of the jungle in my mind, the strongman that kept all other struggles in place.

I found myself asking:

- What woman would want me?
- Who could accept my past?
- How could I be pure enough?
- When would the struggle end?

The Wildlife vs. The Lion

Here's what I learned: You can fight wildlife all day long, but until you confront the lion, the jungle remains unsafe. I was:

- Dealing with temptations but not the root
- Fighting attractions but not the source
- Managing behavior but not the cause
- Controlling actions but not the origin

The Revelation of Authority

But then God showed me something: Just like David, I didn't need to fight every animal in the jungle. I needed to confront the lion. Because when you defeat the king of the jungle:

- Lesser predators flee
- Smaller threats submit
- Weaker enemies scatter
- Lower-level battles cease

The Path to Victory

The breakthrough came when I realized:

1. Identity Beyond Trauma

- I am not my molestation
- I am not my confusion
- I am not my struggles
- I am not my past

2. Authority Over Territory
- My mind is my territory
- My body is my temple
- My future is my promise
- My destiny is my right

The Lion's Defeat

When I finally faced and defeated the lion of perversion:
- Sexual confusion had to bow
- Identity struggles had to submit
- Relationship fears had to flee
- Intimacy barriers had to fall

Why? Because when you defeat the king of the jungle, everything under its authority must recognize your victory.

The Marriage Miracle

This victory opened the door for authentic relationships and eventually marriage. Because now:

- I wasn't bringing wildlife into my marriage
- I wasn't carrying jungle into my covenant
- I wasn't transferring predators into my partnership
- I wasn't importing battles into my bond

The Testimony of Transformation

Today, I stand as living proof that:

- Your molestation is not your destiny
- Your confusion is not your conclusion
- Your struggles are not your story
- Your past is not your prison

A Word to Fellow Survivors

To every person who's been molested, who's battling sexual confusion, who's fighting in their mind:

1. Identify Your Lion

- Name your main battle
- Face your root issue
- Confront your source struggle
- Challenge your primary predator

2. Claim Your Territory

- Your mind is yours
- Your body is yours
- Your future is yours
- Your destiny is yours

3. Exercise Your Authority

- Over thoughts
- Over feelings
- Over memories
- Over triggers

The Promise of Freedom

Remember:

- Victory isn't just possible
- It's your birthright
- Healing isn't just available
- It's your inheritance

You can:

- Move beyond management to mastery

- Shift from coping to conquering
- Transform from surviving to slaying
- Progress from battling to building

The Final Declaration

I declare over every survivor:

- Your lion can be defeated
- Your jungle can be cleared
- Your mind can be freed
- Your future can be claimed

    Because the God who helped David slay his lion

    Is the God who will help you slay yours.

    The authority that worked in my life

    Is available in yours.

    Your molestation is not your master

    Your confusion is not your captain

    Your struggle is not your story

    Your past is not your prison

    Rise up.

    Face your lion.

    Claim your territory.

    Walk in victory.

    Remember: It's not enough to fight the wildlife

    You must slay the lion

    It's not enough to manage the symptoms

WHAT THE FEAR IS GOING ON

You must master the source

Your complete victory awaits

Your total freedom calls

Your perfect peace beckons

Your full healing approaches

Step into it.

Walk in it.

Live from it.

Testify through it.

CHAPTER 9
FEAR OF LOSS

"How long will you mourn for Saul, seeing I have rejected him from reigning over Israel?"
(1 Samuel 16:1)

The Prison of Potential Loss: When Leaders Grieve What Isn't Yet Gone

The Prophet's Pain: Samuel's Journey with Loss

"How long will you mourn for Saul, seeing I have rejected him from reigning over Israel?" (1 Samuel 16:1)

Let me take you into a moment that exposes one of leadership's deepest struggles. Here stands Samuel, a mighty prophet, caught in the grip of grief not just for what was lost, but for what could be lost. This wasn't just sadness – this was a spirit of grief partnering with the fear of loss.

The Anatomy of Leadership Loss

1. Samuel's Struggle

- Mourning a failed investment

- Grieving broken expectations
- Aching over wasted potential
- Fearing future failures

His grief was so profound that God Himself had to intervene. Think about that – the prophet who could see into others' futures was blind to his own next step because grief had clouded his vision.

2. Moses' Battle

Watch Moses at the burning bush:
- Fear of losing credibility
- Fear of losing influence
- Fear of losing respect
- Fear of losing himself

"Who am I that I should go to Pharaoh?" The fear of loss had him negotiating with his own destiny.

3. Elijah's Crisis

After Mount Carmel:
- Fear of losing his life
- Fear of losing his mission
- Fear of losing his impact
- Fear of being alone

"I am the only one left, and now they are trying to kill me too." The fear of loss drove him into isolation and depression.

The Partnership of Fear and Grief

Watch this revelation:

1. **Fear of Loss Breeds Preventive Grief**
   - Grieving before losing
   - Mourning potential losses

- Aching over possible endings
- Suffering future separations

2. **Grief Creates Fear Cycles**
   - Fear of more loss
   - Fear of repeated pain
   - Fear of future attachment
   - Fear of new investment

The Leadership Trap

Many leaders get caught here:

1. **In Ministry**
   - Fear of losing people
   - Fear of losing influence
   - Fear of losing support
   - Fear of losing vision

2. **In Relationships**
   - Fear of losing connection
   - Fear of losing trust
   - Fear of losing loyalty
   - Fear of losing community

3. **In Purpose**
   - Fear of losing direction
   - Fear of losing clarity
   - Fear of losing momentum
   - Fear of losing impact

The Manifestation of Loss Fear

It shows up as:

1. **Control Mechanisms**
   - Over-protection
   - Micro-management
   - Excessive oversight
   - Unhealthy attachment
2. **Emotional Withdrawal**
   - Preemptive distance
   - Emotional walls
   - Relational barriers
   - Heart guards
3. **Ministry Paralysis**
   - Delayed decisions
   - Avoided risks
   - Missed opportunities
   - Stunted growth

God's Intervention with Samuel

Watch God's therapy for a grieving prophet:

1. **The Confrontation**
   - "How long will you mourn?"
   - Questioning the length of grief
   - Challenging the fear's residence
   - Addressing the emotional paralysis
2. **The Direction**
   - "Fill your horn with oil"
   - Commanding new action
   - Initiating new movement
   - Requiring new faith

3. **The Promise**
    - "I have provided Myself a king"
    - Assuring continued purpose
    - Guaranteeing divine provision
    - Confirming future plans

Breaking the Fear-Grief Cycle

1. **Recognize the Pattern**
    - Fear anticipating loss
    - Grief preceding separation
    - Mourning potential endings
    - Suffering future possibilities

2. **Release the Weight**
    - Let go of false responsibility
    - Surrender control anxiety
    - Release attachment fear
    - Abandon failure dread

3. **Receive New Assignment**
    - Embrace fresh direction
    - Accept new purpose
    - Welcome new season
    - Enter new territory

The Victory Pattern in Scripture

Watch how others overcame:

1. **Moses Overcame**
    - Faced his fears
    - Embraced his calling
    - Released his excuses

- Fulfilled his purpose

2. **Elijah Recovered**
   - Heard God's whisper
   - Received new direction
   - Found new companions
   - Continued his mission

3. **Paul Transformed**
   - Lost everything
   - Gained Christ
   - Released past
   - Embraced future

The Leadership Liberation

To break free:

1. **Face Your Fears**
   - Name your loss fears
   - Identify grief triggers
   - Recognize control patterns
   - Admit emotional barriers

2. **Feel Your Feelings**
   - Allow legitimate grief
   - Process real loss
   - Experience true emotion
   - Release false guilt

3. **Follow God's Next**
   - Hear new direction
   - Accept new assignment
   - Embrace new season

- Trust new path

The Promise in Loss

Remember:

1. **God Never Ends on Loss**
   - Every end has purpose
   - Every loss has promise
   - Every grief has growth
   - Every pain has potential

2. **New Begins in Release**
   - Freedom follows surrender
   - Purpose follows pain
   - Direction follows release
   - Assignment follows acceptance

A Prayer for Fearful Leaders

"Father, deliver us from:

- The fear that paralyzes
- The grief that blinds
- The loss that binds
- The control that kills

And give us:

- Faith to release
- Courage to continue
- Strength to start again
- Vision to see Your next"

The Final Word

To every leader trapped in the fear of loss:

- Your grief is seen
- Your fear is understood
- Your pain has purpose
- Your release has reward

But like Samuel:

- It's time to stop mourning what God has closed
- It's time to fill your horn with oil
- It's time to move toward new assignment
- It's time to trust God's next

Because in the kingdom:

- Loss isn't the end
- Grief isn't the conclusion
- Fear isn't the final word
- Change isn't the destroyer

Your next assignment awaits your release of the last one. Your new season requires your goodbye to the old one. Your fresh anointing demands your surrender of the former one.

It's time to let go and move forward. Not in fear, but in faith. Not in grief, but in grace. Not in loss, but in love.

Divine Therapy: Understanding God's Treatment Plan for Grieving Prophets

The Prophetic Burden of Sight

Before we dive into God's therapy, let me speak to something most prophetic people won't admit: The weight of seeing is also the weight of grieving. When God lets you see with His eyes, you also feel with His heart.

"The word of the Lord came to Jeremiah… concerning the grievous things." (Jeremiah 14:1)

The Multi-Layered Nature of Prophetic Grief

1. **Present Grief**
   - What is happening
   - What is manifesting
   - What is breaking
   - What is dying

2. **Future Grief**
   - What will happen
   - What could happen
   - What might fail
   - What might be lost

3. **Redemptive Grief**
   - What could have been
   - What should have been
   - What might have been
   - What was meant to be

God's Therapeutic Approach

1. The Divine Confrontation

"How long will you mourn for Saul?" (1 Samuel 16:1)

Watch the therapy in this question:

a) Time Assessment
- "How long" addresses duration
- Questions the season of grief
- Challenges the length of mourning
- Examines the period of pain

b) Purpose Evaluation
- Why are you mourning?
- What's feeding this grief?
- Where is this leading?
- When will it end?

c) Identity Reminder
- You're a prophet, not just a griever
- You're called, not just caring
- You're purposed, not just paining
- You're assigned, not just aching

2. The Divine Direction

"Fill your horn with oil and go" (1 Samuel 16:1)

Watch the therapy in this command:

a) Practical Action
- Physical movement interrupts emotional paralysis
- Tangible tasks break intangible bonds
- Concrete steps combat abstract pain
- Specific actions heal general grief

b) Symbolic Meaning
- Fill (replenishment after emptiness)
- Horn (authority after weakness)

- Oil (anointing after mourning)
- Go (movement after stagnation)

c) Prophetic Pattern
- Preparation follows pain
- Assignment follows anguish
- Purpose follows grief
- Direction follows loss

3. The Divine Promise

"I have provided Myself a king" (1 Samuel 16:1)

Watch the therapy in this assurance:

a) Divine Provision
- God's "I have" answers prophet's "What if?"
- Heaven's certainty calms earth's anxiety
- Father's provision meets prophet's concern
- Lord's preparation exceeds servant's preparation

b) Future Focus
- New vision beyond old loss
- Fresh purpose beyond past pain
- Coming victory beyond current void
- Future triumph beyond present trauma

Specific Application for Prophetic Offices

1. For Prophetic Intercessors
- Who carry the weight of what could be lost
- Who feel the burden of what might fail
- Who bear the pain of potential destruction

Your Therapy:
- Set prayer boundaries
- Establish emotional borders
- Create intercession timeframes
- Practice release prayers

2. For Prophetic Midwives
- Who assist in spiritual birth
- Who witness transition pain
- Who support through process

Your Therapy:
- Learn holy detachment
- Practice sacred separation
- Maintain spiritual boundaries
- Honor process without absorbing pain

3. For Prophetic Worshipers
- Who feel the depths of spirit
- Who carry atmospheric weight
- Who bear worship warfare

Your Therapy:
- Balance expression and experience
- Alternate between warfare and worship
- Cycle through lament and praise
- Move between crying and celebration

4. For Prophetic Creatives
- Who see what could be
- Who feel what should be
- Who create from pain

Your Therapy:
- Channel grief into creation
- Transform pain into production
- Convert mourning into making
- Translate anguish into art

5. For Prophetic Entrepreneurs
- Who see market mourning
- Who feel economic shifts
- Who carry business burdens

Your Therapy:
- Balance vision and implementation
- Separate personal from profitable
- Distinguish emotion from execution
- Convert burden to business

The Therapeutic Process

1. Divine Assessment

"Search me, O God, and know my heart" (Psalm 139:23)

Watch for:
- Hidden grief points
- Masked pain areas
- Concealed sorrow spots
- Buried trauma zones

2. Divine Treatment

"He heals the brokenhearted and binds up their wounds"
(Psalm 147:3)

Through:
- Word therapy
- Spirit counsel
- Truth treatment
- Grace healing

3. Divine Rehabilitation

"Restore to me the joy of your salvation" (Psalm 51:12)

Including:
- Strength rebuilding
- Vision clearing
- Purpose realigning
- Assignment resuming

Prophetic Protocols for Healing

1. Acknowledgment Phase
- - Name your grief
- - Face your loss
- - Admit your pain
- - Accept your process

2. Processing Phase
- - Feel your feelings
- - Express your emotions
- - Release your burdens
- - Share your struggles

3. Transition Phase
- - Embrace new direction
- - Accept fresh assignment
- - Welcome next season
- - Enter new territory

The Promise to Grieving Prophets

Remember:

1. **Your Grief is Not Forever**
   - Seasons change
   - Assignments shift
   - Purpose evolves
   - Direction moves

2. **Your Pain Has Purpose**
   - Grief develops compassion
   - Loss increases capacity
   - Pain deepens ministry
   - Anguish expands authority

3. **Your Next is Protected**
   - God has provided
   - Heaven has prepared
   - Spirit has planned
   - Father has purposed

The Prophetic Promise

To every grieving prophet:
- Your mourning will turn to morning
- Your weeping will wake to working
- Your pain will transform to purpose

- Your grief will grow into glory

Because divine therapy isn't just about healing; It's about reforming. It's not just about recovery; It's about repositioning.

Your grief isn't your grave; It's your graduation. Your pain isn't your prison; It's your preparation.

Let the Divine Therapist do His work. Let the Heavenly Counselor complete His process. Let the Spirit Comforter fulfill His purpose.

For after grief comes glory, After mourning comes mission, After pain comes purpose, After loss comes legacy.

Specialized Divine Therapy: For Prophetic Marriages, Ministries, and Pastors

For Prophetic Marriages

The Unique Burden

When both partners carry prophetic mantles, they face:
- Double portion of spiritual weight
- Amplified sensitivity to spiritual atmosphere
- Multiplied burden of vision
- Intensified warfare against union

Watch this: In prophetic marriages, you're dealing with:

1. **Compound Sight**
   - Both partners seeing
   - Both partners feeling
   - Both partners carrying
   - Both partners processing

2. **Amplified Grief Points**
   - Personal grief
   - Partner's grief

- Shared grief
- Ministry grief

Divine Marriage Therapy

1. **Boundary Setting**
    - Establish grief-free zones
    - Create prophetic pause periods
    - Maintain intimate spaces without ministry
    - Define when to carry and when to release

2. **Communication Protocols**
    - Share burden without transferring it
    - Express vision without imposing it
    - Process grief without projecting it
    - Release weight without dumping it

3. **Unity Maintenance**
    - Guard intimate connection
    - Protect marriage covenant
    - Preserve personal space
    - Maintain couple identity

For Prophetic Ministries

The Organizational Weight

Prophetic ministries carry:

- Corporate burden
- Collective vision
- Community weight
- Kingdom mandate

The Unique Challenges

1. **Atmospheric Management**
   - Maintaining hope while seeing trouble
   - Balancing warning and worship
   - Managing revelation and rejoicing
   - Combining prophecy and praise

2. **Team Dynamics**
   - Leading through heaviness
   - Guiding through grief
   - Directing through difficulty
   - Stewarding through sorrow

Divine Ministry Therapy

1. **Structural Implementation**
   - Build grief processing systems
   - Create revelation release protocols
   - Establish burden bearing boundaries
   - Design prophetic development paths

2. **Team Care Protocols**
   - Regular debriefing sessions
   - Scheduled renewal periods
   - Intentional celebration times
   - Purposeful praise moments

3. **Vision Maintenance**
   - Keep hope visible
   - Hold promise prominent
   - Maintain joy central
   - Preserve purpose clear

For Prophetic Pastors

The Dual Mantle Weight

Carrying both:

- Pastoral care burden
- Prophetic sight burden
- Shepherd's heart weight
- Seer's vision weight

The Unique Tension

1. **Between Seeing and Shepherding**
   - Knowing what's coming but nurturing present peace
   - Seeing future challenges but maintaining current calm
   - Carrying coming change but cultivating current stability
   - Holding heaven's perspective while handling earth's process

2. **Between Warning and Comforting**
   - When to speak and when to shelter
   - When to reveal and when to protect
   - When to challenge and when to comfort
   - When to push and when to pause

Divine Pastoral Therapy

1. **Personal Maintenance**

Prayer Strategy:

- Morning mercy receiving
- Midday burden releasing
- Evening glory reflecting
- Night peace securing

2. **Ministry Management**

Wisdom Protocol:

- Balance revelation with relationship
- Merge prophecy with pastoral care
- Combine vision with nurture
- Unite truth with tenderness

3. **Burden Bearing Boundaries**

Protection Plan:

- Define carrying capacity
- Establish release times
- Create processing spaces
- Maintain renewal rhythms

The Promise for Each

For Prophetic Marriages

> *"Though one may be overpowered, two can defend themselves. A cord of three strands is not quickly broken." (Ecclesiastes 4:12)*

Your Promise:

- United sight brings united might
- Shared burden becomes shared blessing
- Combined grief transforms to combined glory
- Mutual carrying leads to mutual crowning

For Prophetic Ministries

> *"And I will give you shepherds according to My heart, who will feed you with knowledge and understanding." (Jeremiah 3:15)*

Your Promise:

- Heavy revelation becomes heavy blessing
- Deep burden produces deep impact
- Strong grief creates strong ministry
- Great weight leads to great glory

For Prophetic Pastors

> *"He will feed His flock like a shepherd; He will gather the lambs with His arm." (Isaiah 40:11)*

Your Promise:

- Dual mantle brings dual blessing
- Combined calling creates combined impact
- Merged gifts produce merged glory
- United purpose yields united power

   To all carrying these unique mantles:

   Your grief is not just grief It's graduation ground.

   Your burden is not just weight It's birthing ground.

   Your heaviness is not just pressure It's preparation ground.

Remember:

- God sees the weight
- Heaven knows the burden

- Spirit understands the pressure
- Father honors the carrying

Therefore:

Let Him heal your hearts.

Let Him restore your strength.

Let Him renew your vision.

Let Him refresh your purpose.

For after this grief Comes greater glory.

After this carrying Comes clearer calling.

After this weight Comes wider influence.

The Divine Therapist is at work.

The Heavenly Healer is engaged.

The Spirit Comforter is moving.

The Father's love is healing.

Holy Release: Understanding the Sacred Art of Prophetic Surrender

The Anatomy of Holy Release

Let me break down something that most prophetic people struggle to understand: There's a difference between carrying and keeping. God never intended for us to permanently store what He temporarily gives us to carry.

"Cast your burden upon the LORD, and He shall sustain you"
(Psalm 55:22)

The Three Dimensions of Holy Release

1. Prophetic Release

This is releasing what you've seen:

- Visions that burden
- Dreams that weigh
- Revelations that heavy
- Insights that overwhelm

Watch this principle: Just as Moses had to speak to the rock, there's a time to release the word you've been carrying. Holding it too long turns revelation into resistance.

2. Intercessory Release

This is releasing what you've carried:

- Burdens for others
- Weights for nations
- Concerns for churches
- Prayers for people

"And Hannah prayed… and said: 'My heart rejoices in the Lord'" (1 Samuel 2:1) Notice: After years of carrying the burden for a son, she had to release both the burden and the blessing.

3. Pastoral Release

This is releasing what you've held:

- People's pain
- Others' grief
- Community trauma
- Corporate burdens

The Technology of Holy Release

1. The Timing Element

Divine Schedule:

- Morning release (Yesterday's burdens)
- Midday release (Accumulated weight)
- Evening release (Day's downloading)
- Night release (Final surrender)

2. The Method Element

Sacred Process:

- Identify the burden
- Acknowledge its purpose
- Complete its assignment
- Release its weight

3. The Location Element

Holy Spaces:

- Personal altar
- Prayer closet
- Worship sanctuary
- Nature sanctuary

The Manifestation of Unholy Holding

Watch what happens when we don't practice holy release:

1. **Physical Manifestations**
   - Exhaustion
   - Illness
   - Weakness

- Depletion

2. **Spiritual Manifestations**
   - Blocked revelation
   - Diminished sensitivity
   - Clouded discernment
   - Weakened prophecy

3. **Emotional Manifestations**
   - Overwhelming grief
   - Constant heaviness
   - Persistent sadness
   - Unending burden

The Protocol of Holy Release

1. The Recognition Phase

Ask yourself:

- Is this mine to carry?
- Is this mine to keep?
- Is this season complete?
- Is this burden current?

2. The Release Ceremony

Sacred Steps:

1. Acknowledge the weight
2. Honor its purpose
3. Declare its completion
4. Release its authority

3. The Renewal Process

After Release:

1. Receive fresh strength

2. Accept new capacity

3. Welcome new burden

4. Embrace new season

The Prophetic Pattern of Release

Watch this in Scripture:

1. **Elijah's Pattern**
    - Carried the burden
    - Delivered the word
    - Released the weight
    - Received new assignment

2. **Samuel's Pattern**
    - Grieved for Saul
    - Heard God's timing
    - Released the grief
    - Embraced new direction

3. **Daniel's Pattern**
    - Carried revelation
    - Delivered interpretation
    - Released responsibility
    - Received more wisdom

The Divine Design in Release

Understand this principle:

1. **God's Economy of Burden**
   - He gives weight to develop strength
   - He allows burden to build capacity
   - He permits carrying to increase authority
   - He requires release to maintain health

2. **Heaven's Flow of Revelation**
   - Receive
   - Carry
   - Deliver
   - Release

3. **Spirit's Cycle of Ministry**
   - Accept assignment
   - Complete purpose
   - Release weight
   - Await next

The Warning Signs of Unholy Holding

Watch for these indicators:

1. **In Prayer Life**
   - Repetitive prayers
   - Stale intercession
   - Blocked revelation
   - Diminished authority

2. **In Prophetic Flow**
   - Recycled words
   - Old revelations
   - Stuck messages
   - Past seasons

3. **In Personal Life**
   - Continuous exhaustion
   - Persistent heaviness
   - Constant overwhelm
   - Unending grief

The Promise in Holy Release

Remember:

1. **Release Creates Capacity**
   - For new revelation
   - For fresh burden
   - For greater authority
   - For deeper insight

2. **Surrender Enables Supply**
   - New strength comes
   - Fresh grace flows
   - Added power arrives
   - Increased clarity emerges

3. **Letting Go Leads to Lifting Up**
   - Higher revelation
   - Deeper understanding
   - Clearer vision
   - Stronger authority

The Prophetic Declaration for Release

Declare:

"I release:
   - What was for then

- What's complete now
- What's fulfilled here
- What's finished today

I receive:
- Fresh capacity
- New authority
- Greater revelation
- Deeper insight"

The Final Word on Holy Release

Understand:
- Release isn't rejection
- Surrender isn't failure
- Letting go isn't losing
- Releasing isn't retreating

It's:
- Making room for more
- Creating space for new
- Preparing for next
- Positioning for greater

Your release is your reset

Your surrender is your setup

Your letting go is your lifting up

Your goodbye is your gateway

Practice holy release:

Not just to be free from

But to be free for

Not just to be empty of

But to be filled with

For in God's kingdom:

Every release creates capacity

Every surrender enables supply

Every letting go leads to lifting up

Every holy release enables holy receiving

CHAPTER 10
FEAR OF ISOLATION

The path of leadership is rarely a solitary one. Leaders often find themselves at the helm, making critical decisions that affect the lives and livelihoods of those around them. But there's a dark side to this position of authority. It's a side that can leave even the most confident and capable leaders feeling isolated and alone.

This is what we call the "Lone Leader Syndrome" – a phenomenon where leaders, especially those in senior positions, experience a sense of isolation and a lack of genuine connection with others. It's a silent struggle that can manifest in various ways. Leaders might find themselves withdrawing from their teams, hesitant to share their vulnerabilities, or battling with the weight of their decisions in the absence of a trusted confidant.

The roots of the Lone Leader Syndrome run deep. Often, it stems from the perceived need for leaders to appear strong, infallible, and always in control. They may feel pressured to project an image of unwavering confidence, fearing that showing vulnerability or seeking support will undermine their authority. This fear of appearing weak can lead to a vicious cycle of isolation.

This sense of isolation can be particularly acute when leaders are faced with difficult decisions. These are times when doubt and uncertainty naturally surface, yet the pressure to maintain a facade of confidence can make it challenging for leaders to seek advice or support. They may fear that confiding in others will be perceived as weakness, or that it will undermine their ability to make tough calls. But the truth is, no leader is an island. Even the most experienced and seasoned leaders need support. And when leaders isolate themselves, they deprive themselves of invaluable insights, perspectives, and emotional support that can help them navigate challenges, make sound decisions, and ultimately, lead more effectively.

Here are a few factors that can contribute to the Lone Leader Syndrome:

The Myth of the Lone Ranger:

The popular culture often portrays leaders as solitary heroes, operating independently and taking on challenges single-handedly. This romanticized image can reinforce the idea that leaders should be self-sufficient and avoid seeking support.

Fear of Losing Control:

Leaders may fear that seeking advice or sharing their concerns with others will weaken their control over decisions and outcomes. They may worry that losing control will be perceived as a sign of weakness.

Lack of Trust and Open Communication:

A culture of distrust or closed communication within an organization can make it difficult for leaders to feel comfortable sharing their vulnerabilities with their teams.

High Expectations and Pressure to Perform:

Leaders often face enormous pressure to deliver results, meet deadlines, and exceed expectations. This relentless pressure can contribute to feelings of isolation and the need to carry the burden of leadership alone.

Lack of Mentorship and Support:

Some leaders may not have access to mentors or support systems that can provide guidance, encouragement, and a sense of belonging.

The consequences of the Lone Leader Syndrome can be significant. It can lead to:

Poor Decision-Making:

Leaders who feel isolated may make decisions based on limited information or their own biases, without seeking diverse perspectives.

Reduced Creativity and Innovation:

A sense of isolation can stifle creativity, as leaders may hesitate to share ideas or take risks for fear of judgment.

Increased Stress and Burnout:

The constant pressure to perform and the absence of support can lead to increased stress levels, burnout, and decreased job satisfaction.

Decreased Team Morale and Productivity:

When leaders feel isolated, their teams may also feel disconnected, lacking a sense of purpose or direction.

The good news is that the Lone Leader Syndrome is not an inevitable consequence of leadership. Leaders can take proactive steps to combat this isolation and build stronger connections:

Embrace Vulnerability:

Leaders can set a positive example by being willing to share their vulnerabilities and challenges with their teams. This demonstrates authenticity, encourages open communication, and creates a more supportive environment.

Seek Mentorship and Support:

Leaders should proactively seek out mentors and support systems, both inside and outside their organizations. This provides a space for reflection, guidance, and emotional support.

Build Strong Relationships:

Leaders can cultivate authentic relationships with team members, colleagues, and peers by engaging in open communication, actively listening, and showing empathy.

Create a Culture of Trust and Open Communication:

Leaders can foster a culture where team members feel comfortable sharing ideas, providing feedback, and seeking support. This requires creating a safe environment where everyone feels heard and valued.

Delegate and Empower Others:

Leaders can combat isolation by delegating tasks and empowering team members to take on leadership roles. This builds trust, fosters collaboration, and allows leaders to share the burden of responsibility.

Prioritize Self-Care:

Leaders must prioritize their own well-being by engaging in activities that promote physical and mental health. This might include exercise, mindfulness practices, or spending time with loved ones.

Remember, leadership is not a solitary pursuit. It's a journey that requires collaboration, support, and genuine human connection. By embracing vulnerability, seeking mentorship, and cultivating strong relationships, leaders can overcome the Lone Leader Syndrome and build a culture of trust, innovation, and resilience.

The Isolation Paradox: Understanding Divine Separation vs. Demonic Isolation

The Prophet's Cave: Elijah's Journey with Loneliness

"I am the only one left, and now they are trying to kill me too."
(1 Kings 19:14)

Let me take you to a cave where one of God's most powerful leaders sat in isolation, so convinced of his aloneness that he wished for death. This wasn't just physical isolation – this was soul-deep loneliness.

The Leadership Loneliness Crisis

Let's be real about something that most leaders won't admit:

1. **The Weight of Alone**
   - Empty hotel rooms after powerful conferences
   - Quiet car rides after dynamic services
   - Silent nights after public victories
   - Solitary moments after shared triumphs

2. **The Cost of Position**
   - Few understand your burden
   - Many want your platform
   - Some share your vision
   - None carry your weight

Divine Isolation vs. Demonic Isolation

Watch this revelation:

Divine Isolation:

1. **Purpose Driven**
   - For preparation
   - For purification
   - For revelation
   - For elevation

2. **Time Limited**
   - Has a start point
   - Has an end point

- Has a purpose
- Has a product

Demonic Isolation:

1. **Fear Driven**
   - Creates paranoia
   - Breeds suspicion
   - Fosters mistrust
   - Generates anxiety

2. **Perpetual**
   - Never enough connection
   - Never enough community
   - Never enough support
   - Never enough presence

The Enemy's Strategy in Isolation

Satan uses isolation to:

1. **Distort Perspective**
   - "I'm the only one"
   - "No one understands"
   - "I'm alone in this"
   - "Nobody else gets it"

2. **Destroy Purpose**
   - Through discouragement
   - Through depression
   - Through despair
   - Through defeat

God's Strategy in Separation

The Lord uses separation to:

1. **Develop Character**
   - Private integrity
   - Personal strength
   - Inner fortitude
   - Core values

2. **Deepen Connection**
   - With His presence
   - With His purpose
   - With His power
   - With His plan

Elijah's Cave Experience

Watch the progression:

1. **The Isolation**
   - After great victory
   - During intense warfare
   - Amidst death threats
   - Through personal fear

2. **The Depression**
   - Wanted to die
   - Felt alone
   - Lost perspective
   - Forgot victory

3. **The Divine Response**
   - Still small voice
   - New assignment

- Hidden companions
- Future promise

The Hidden Company

> *"Yet I reserve seven thousand in Israel—all whose knees have not bowed down to Baal" (1 Kings 19:18)*

God's revelation to Elijah:

1. **You're Not Alone**
   - Others exist
   - Others remain
   - Others stand
   - Others believe

2. **They're Hidden**
   - For protection
   - For preparation
   - For purpose
   - For positioning

Modern Leadership Application

For today's leaders:

1. **Recognize the Season**

Ask yourself:
- Is this divine separation?
- Or demonic isolation?
- Is this preparation?
- Or persecution?

2. **Respond Appropriately**

If Divine:
- Embrace the process
- Extract the purpose
- Engage the presence
- Expect the promotion

If Demonic:
- Resist the lie
- Reject the loneliness
- Reach for connection
- Restore perspective

The Isolation Process

Understanding the journey:

1. **Entry Phase**
   - Separation begins
   - Crowd diminishes
   - Support reduces
   - Loneliness enters

2. **Development Phase**
   - Character builds
   - Strength grows
   - Faith deepens
   - Purpose clarifies

3. **Victory Phase**
   - Perspective shifts
   - Purpose emerges
   - Power increases

- Position elevates

Leadership Promises in Isolation

Remember:

1. **Divine Positioning**
   - Isolation elevates
   - Separation promotes
   - Solitude prepares
   - Aloneness advances

2. **Hidden Purpose**
   - In every silence
   - In every separation
   - In every solitude
   - In every isolation

A Word to Isolated Leaders

Understand:
- Your cave is not your coffin
- Your isolation is not your extinction
- Your solitude is not your sentence
- Your separation is not your conclusion

Remember:
- Moses had a backside of the desert
- David had a wilderness
- Paul had an Arabia
- Jesus had a wilderness

The Promise in Isolation

Your isolation is:

- Not punishment but preparation
- Not rejection but repositioning
- Not abandonment but advancement
- Not defeat but development

While the enemy uses isolation to:
- Break you
- Defeat you
- Destroy you
- Diminish you

God uses isolation to:
- Build you
- Strengthen you
- Prepare you
- Position you

To every isolated leader:
- Your cave has a purpose
- Your solitude has significance
- Your separation has strategy
- Your isolation has intent

Don't fight the isolation, Navigate it. Don't resist the separation, Maximize it

Because after isolation comes:
- Greater authority
- Deeper impact
- Stronger influence
- Wider reach

Your isolation isn't your end. It's your elevator. Your separation isn't your defeat. It's your development.

Stay in the process. Trust the progression. Honor the preparation. Await the promotion.

For after this isolation Comes elevation After this separation Comes celebration.

The Sacred Space of Being Hidden: When Preparation Looks Nothing Like the Promise

The Karate Kid Principle

Let me break something down for you. Remember Mr. Miyagi having Daniel-san wax cars, paint fences, and sand floors? To Daniel, these tasks seemed disconnected from his desire to learn karate. But watch this revelation:

1. **Wax On, Wax Off**
    - Looked like: Menial labor
    - Building: Muscle memory
    - Developing: Defensive techniques
    - Creating: Foundational movements

2. **Paint the Fence**
    - Appeared as: Household chores
    - Installing: Blocking techniques
    - Establishing: Protective reflexes
    - Forming: Fighting instincts

My Hidden Seasons Journey

Let me testify:

1. **The McDonald's Season**
    - Position: Crew Trainer

- Learning: People management
- Developing: Systems thinking
- Building: Leadership skills

2. **The Drummer Season**
   - Role: Church musician
   - Learning: Team synchronization
   - Developing: Spiritual sensitivity
   - Building: Ministry timing

3. **The Sunday School Season**
   - Task: Teaching children
   - Learning: Scripture communication
   - Developing: Pastoral heart
   - Building: Spiritual nurturing

The Purpose of Hidden Places

Watch this principle:

1. **Hidden Doesn't Mean Inactive**
   - It means intentional development
   - It means protected growth
   - It means guided formation
   - It means purposeful preparation

2. **Hidden Doesn't Mean Forgotten**
   - It means preserved
   - It means protected
   - It means prepared
   - It means positioned

Biblical Hidden Seasons

1. **Joseph's Journey**
   - The pit season
   - The Potiphar season
   - The prison season
   - Each preparing for the palace

2. **David's Development**
   - The shepherd season
   - The servant season
   - The soldier season
   - Each preparing for sovereignty

3. **Moses' Maturation**
   - The palace learning
   - The wilderness waiting
   - The backside developing
   - Each preparing for prophecy

The Technology of Hidden Preparation

1. Skill Development

Visible Task → Hidden Lesson

Mundane Work → Mighty Preparation

Regular Routine → Royal Training

Daily Duties → Divine Development

2. Character Formation

Process Purpose:
   - Humility through hiddenness

- Patience through process
- Strength through struggle
- Wisdom through waiting

The Danger of Premature Emergence

Watch what happens when we fight being hidden:

1. **Character Casualties**
    - Undeveloped humility
    - Untested integrity
    - Unformed wisdom
    - Unestablished strength

2. **Leadership Liabilities**
    - Weak foundations
    - Shallow roots
    - Limited capacity
    - Unstable authority

The Hidden Season Curriculum

Your hidden season is teaching you:

1. **Leadership Foundations**
    - People management
    - Resource stewardship
    - Vision development
    - Team building

2. **Character Essentials**
    - Humility in service
    - Excellence in small things
    - Faithfulness in monotony

- Diligence in development

The Promise in Being Hidden

Remember:

1. **Every Hidden Season**
   - Has purpose
   - Has process
   - Has plan
   - Has promotion

2. **Every Mundane Moment**
   - Builds something
   - Develops something
   - Creates something
   - Prepares something

The Principles of Emergence

Understanding when it's time:

1. **Character Indicators**
   - Humility is established
   - Excellence is automatic
   - Service is natural
   - Leadership is earned

2. **Skill Markers**
   - Foundation is solid
   - Expertise is proven
   - Authority is earned
   - Influence is natural

A Word to Hidden Leaders

To those in their hidden season:

1. **Embrace the Process**
    - Honor small beginnings
    - Value current lessons
    - Respect present training
    - Cherish hidden growth

2. **Trust the Preparation**
    - Every task has purpose
    - Every role has reason
    - Every position prepares
    - Every season shapes

The Hidden Season Declaration

Declare over your hidden season:

"I am not just:
- A crew trainer but a leader in training
- A drummer but a minister in development
- A teacher but a shepherd in preparation
- A servant but a ruler in formation"

The Power of Hidden Development

Understand:
- Hidden doesn't mean halted
- Concealed doesn't mean canceled
- Unseen doesn't mean unimportant
- Private doesn't mean purposeless

Your hidden season is:

- Not denying your destiny
- But developing your capacity
- Not delaying your purpose
- But deepening your preparation

Final Words of Wisdom

Remember:
- Don't rush emergence
- Don't fight hiddenness
- Don't resist preparation
- Don't neglect development

Because:
- What's hidden will be revealed
- What's concealed will be unveiled
- What's developing will be displayed
- What's preparing will be promoted

Your hidden season isn't:
- A punishment to endure
- A sentence to serve
- A delay to survive
- A detour to resent

It's:
- A foundational time
- A formational space
- A developmental place
- A preparational grace

Embrace being hidden Honor the process Trust the preparation Await the emergence

For when the season shifts:
- Your preparation will prove purposeful
- Your development will demonstrate destiny
- Your hiddenness will herald honor
- Your patience will produce promotion

CHAPTER 11
FEAR OF SUCCESS

The Weight of Winning - My Story: The Cost of Rising

Let me take you into a struggle that most leaders won't admit to – the fear of success. Not failure, but success. Success that would make me different. Success that would set me apart. Success that would make me, in some ways, alone.

As I climbed the corporate ladder to CFO and expanded in ministry, I found myself wrestling with something I never expected: the weight of becoming what no one in my family had become before. It wasn't just about achievement – it was about identity, belonging, and the cost of breaking new ground.

The Family Dynamic

Every new level brought new tension:

- Executive meetings where I was the only one from my background
- Family gatherings where my success made others uncomfortable
- Ministry platforms where my corporate success created distance
- Professional spaces where my ministry calling raised eyebrows

I found myself walking a tightrope between worlds, trying to balance:

- Corporate excellence without seeming "too good"

- Ministry impact without appearing "too big"
- Financial success without looking "too different"
- Personal growth without becoming "too distant"

The Hidden Battle

What people didn't see was the internal war:

- Downplaying achievements to make others comfortable
- Hiding blessings to avoid creating distance
- Minimizing impact to maintain relationships
- Reducing visibility to preserve connections

I discovered that what I called "humility" was often fear in disguise:

- Fear of standing out
- Fear of being misunderstood
- Fear of losing connection
- Fear of others' perceptions

The Family First Generation

Being a first-generation success carrier came with unique challenges:

- No roadmap from family experience
- No mentors from similar backgrounds
- No understanding from familiar circles
- No celebration from comfortable spaces

I learned that when you're the first:

- Your success can feel like others' indictment
- Your progress can feel like others' failure
- Your growth can feel like others' loss
- Your elevation can feel like others' reduction

The Perception Battle

The hardest part wasn't achieving success – it was managing how others perceived it. I watched as:

- Family members interpreted ambition as arrogance
- Friends mistook progress for pride
- Colleagues confused excellence for exclusion
- Ministry peers misread influence for ego

Breaking Through

The breakthrough came when I realized:

- My success wasn't about me
- My elevation wasn't for me
- My influence wasn't because of me
- My impact wasn't limited to me

God showed me that:

- Others' perception of my success was their mirror, not my reality
- Their interpretation of my journey was their lens, not my truth
- Their response to my growth was their issue, not my burden
- Their reaction to my elevation was their battle, not my war

The Biblical Pattern

I found comfort in Scripture's success stories:

Joseph's Journey

- Favored child became resented brother
- Successful servant became envied leader
- Elevated prisoner became misunderstood ruler Yet his success served divine purpose

David's Development
- Anointed shepherd became threatening warrior
- Celebrated leader became king's enemy
- Successful king became nation's light Yet his elevation fulfilled heaven's plan

Daniel's Distinction
- Captive youth became government leader
- Foreign advisor became chief administrator
- Faithful believer became kingdom authority Yet his excellence glorified God

The Leadership Lesson

I learned that:

1. **Success Has Purpose**
   - Beyond personal achievement
   - Beyond family legacy
   - Beyond cultural barriers
   - Beyond comfortable limits

2. **Fear Limits Legacy**
   - Reducing impact
   - Restricting influence
   - Restraining purpose
   - Resisting destiny

The Truth About Success Fear

Research shows:

- 70% of leaders battle Imposter Syndrome
- 65% struggle with success-related anxiety
- 75% fear others' reactions to their achievement
- 80% downplay their accomplishments

But here's what I discovered:

- Success isn't selfish if it serves
- Achievement isn't arrogant if it assists
- Excellence isn't ego if it elevates
- Impact isn't pride if it provides

My Message to Rising Leaders

From my journey, I want to tell you:

1. **Own Your Assignment**
   - Your success has purpose
   - Your elevation has meaning
   - Your influence has impact
   - Your achievement has assignment

2. **Accept Your Difference**
   - Being set apart isn't wrong
   - Being different isn't bad
   - Being unique isn't pride
   - Being elevated isn't sin

3. **Embrace Your Impact**
   - Don't diminish your light
   - Don't reduce your influence
   - Don't hide your excellence
   - Don't fear your success

The Freedom Declaration

Today, I declare:

- I will not fear my success
- I will not apologize for my excellence

- I will not hide my impact
- I will not diminish my influence

Because:

- My success serves others
- My elevation enables impact
- My influence creates change
- My achievement opens doors

To every leader battling the fear of success:

- Your achievement isn't arrogance
- Your elevation isn't ego
- Your impact isn't pride
- Your influence isn't selfish

Rise. Achieve. Succeed. Impact.

Not for self-glory But for divine purpose Not for personal praise But for kingdom impact

Your success isn't just about you It's about who you help elevate It's not just about what you achieve It's about who you help succeed

Don't let the fear of success Rob the world of your impact Don't let the fear of perception Steal your divine assignment

Step fully into who you're becoming Embrace fully what you're achieving Accept completely how you're impacting Own thoroughly why you're succeeding

Because someone needs:

- The door you'll open
- The path you'll create
- The ceiling you'll break
- The way you'll make

The Identity Negotiation: When Fear Makes You Trade Who You Are for Who They'll Accept

The Silent Surrender

Let me tell you about a battle that happens in the quiet of successful leaders' hearts – the constant negotiation between who God made you to be and who others will tolerate you being.

The Daily Deals We Make

I found myself making these deals:

- "I'll speak less powerfully so they won't feel threatened"
- "I'll dress down so they won't think I'm showing off"
- "I'll hide my achievements so they won't feel inferior"
- "I'll minimize my influence so they won't feel small"

Watch this dangerous progression:

1. **The Subtle Shifts**
    - Powerful becomes palatable
    - Excellence becomes acceptable
    - Influence becomes invisible
    - Impact becomes ignorable

2. **The Identity Trade**
    - Exchanging authenticity for acceptance
    - Trading purpose for peace
    - Swapping calling for comfort
    - Bartering anointing for approval

The Cost of Negotiation

Here's what happens when you negotiate your identity:

1. **You Lose Yourself**
   - Piece by piece
   - Layer by layer
   - Gift by gift
   - Calling by calling
2. **You Miss Your Mark**
   - Purpose gets diluted
   - Vision gets blurred
   - Impact gets reduced
   - Influence gets limited

The Identity Crisis

Watch how it manifests:

1. **Multiple Versions of You**
   - Corporate you
   - Church you
   - Family you
   - Friend you

   But none of them fully you.

2. **Constant Performance**
   - Adjusting to audiences
   - Shifting for settings
   - Changing for crowds
   - Morphing for moments

The Biblical Warning

"No man can serve two masters" (Matthew 6:24) This isn't just about God and money – it's about identity and authenticity.

Watch these biblical examples:

1. **Saul's Compromise**
   - Called to be king
   - Lived for approval
   - Lost his identity
   - Forfeited his destiny

2. **Peter's Temporary Crisis**
   - Bold with Jesus
   - Fearful with critics
   - Different with Gentiles
   - Changed with Jews

The Identity Theft

The enemy's strategy:

1. **Make You Question**
   - Your authenticity
   - Your authority
   - Your anointing
   - Your assignment

2. **Make You Negotiate**
   - Your expression
   - Your excellence
   - Your impact
   - Your influence

The Real Cost

When you negotiate your identity:

1. **You Rob Others Of**
   - Your full gift
   - Your true impact
   - Your real influence
   - Your authentic presence
2. **You Rob God Of**
   - His complete vessel
   - His prepared instrument
   - His chosen voice
   - His appointed agent

The Authenticity Mandate

Remember:

1. **God Made You**
   - Distinctly
   - Purposefully
   - Intentionally
   - Specifically
2. **You're Called to Be**
   - Fully you
   - Completely you
   - Authentically you
   - Uniquely you

The Identity Recovery

To reclaim your authentic self:

No more:
   - – Dimming your light

- - Reducing your impact
- - Hiding your excellence
- - Minimizing your influence

2. Start the Declarations

I am:

- - Called to excellence
- - Created for impact
- - Designed for influence
- - Made for greatness

The Freedom Protocol

To break free:

1. **Face the Fear**
    - Of being fully seen
    - Of being misunderstood
    - Of being rejected
    - Of being different

2. **Embrace the Truth**
    - Your difference is your design
    - Your uniqueness is your weapon
    - Your authenticity is your authority
    - Your distinctiveness is your destiny

The Leadership Warning

Understand:

- Every negotiation costs
- Every compromise reduces
- Every adjustment diminishes

- Every trade depletes

The Identity Declaration

"I will be:

- Fully who God made me
- Completely who He called me
- Authentically who He designed me
- Uniquely who He purposed me"

A Word to Identity Negotiators

Stop:

- Bargaining with your brilliance
- Trading your treasure
- Negotiating your nature
- Compromising your calling

Remember:

- Your authenticity is your authority
- Your uniqueness is your power
- Your difference is your destiny
- Your distinctiveness is your design

The Final Word

To every leader in identity crisis:

Don't let:

- Fear define you
- Others confine you
- Perception design you
- Acceptance refine you

Your identity is:

- Not up for negotiation
- Not open for discussion
- Not available for trade
- Not subject to approval

Be:

- Unapologetically you
- Unashamedly excellent
- Unabashedly influential
- Uncompromisingly authentic

Because:

- The world needs your voice
- The kingdom needs your gift
- The people need your impact
- The season needs your authentic self

Stop negotiating who you are For who they'll accept Stop trading what you carry For what they'll receive Stop reducing what you bring For what they'll allow

Rise up in your full identity Step into your complete calling Walk in your total anointing Live in your authentic truth

Because you can't fulfill:

- A destiny you're negotiating
- A purpose you're trading
- A calling you're compromising
- An assignment you're adjusting

Be fully, completely, authentically, powerfully YOU.

That's not pride. That's purpose. That's not arrogance. That's assignment.

CHAPTER 12
DO IT SCARED, BUT FEARLESS!

The Final Call to Courageous Leadership

Let me speak a final word to every leader who's been walking with me through this journey of understanding fear. There's something you need to grasp, something that's going to set you free from the paralysis that's been holding you back: Being scared and being fearful are two completely different things.

Being scared is a moment – a natural human response to stepping into unknown territory, facing unprecedented challenges, or walking into divine assignment. Every leader who's ever done anything significant has felt scared. Moses was scared when God called him to face Pharaoh. David was scared when he faced Goliath. Esther was scared when she approached the king's throne. Being scared is not a sin; it's a sign. It's often a signal that you're on the edge of something significant, something destiny-altering, something God-ordained.

But being fearful? That's different. Fearfulness is a state of being, a lens through which you view life, a governor that limits your movements and restricts your obedience. Fearfulness isn't just feeling scared; it's allowing that scared feeling to become your master, your counselor, your guide. It's letting that momentary emotion dictate your permanent position. This is what God warns us against when He says

He hasn't given us a spirit of fear. He's not talking about never feeling scared; He's talking about not living governed by fear.

Let me tell you something that might shake you: Some of the most successful leaders in every sphere - ministry, business, government, education - are still doing it scared. They haven't waited for the feeling of fear to disappear before they moved forward. They've learned to move with knees knocking, with hearts pounding, with hands shaking - but they've moved. They've understood that courage isn't the absence of fear; it's the decision to move forward in the presence of fear.

Right now, in this season, God is raising up a company of leaders who understand this distinction. These are leaders who will feel the fear of stepping into new territory but won't be controlled by it. They're going to launch businesses scared. They're going to start ministries scared. They're going to step into new positions scared. They're going to write books scared. They're going to speak on platforms scared. But they're going to do it anyway, because they understand that their assignment is bigger than their anxiety.

The world is waiting for leaders who have this revelation - that being scared doesn't disqualify you from being powerful. In fact, sometimes it's the scared steps that carry the most weight, because they're steps of pure faith, unmixed with confidence in your own ability. When you move forward scared, you're demonstrating a trust in God that's deeper than your trust in your own emotions. You're declaring that His word is more reliable than your feelings, His promises more trustworthy than your fears.

Think about this: Every giant-killer in Scripture felt scared. Every water-walker felt scared. Every Red Sea-parter felt scared. Every lion's den-survivor felt scared. But they weren't fearful. They didn't let that scared feeling become their identity or their excuse. They converted their scared energy into forward motion, their anxious energy into actionable steps, their nervous energy into noble pursuit.

To every leader reading these words: Your time of hiding behind fear is over. Your season of using fear as an excuse is finished. Your period of waiting until you're not scared is done. God is calling you to a new level of leadership that doesn't deny the presence of scared feelings but refuses to be governed by them. He's calling you to do it scared - to launch scared, to build scared, to speak scared, to lead scared - but to do it anyway.

Remember this: The impact God has assigned to your life is too important to wait until you feel completely fearless. Someone needs what you carry. Someone needs your voice. Someone needs your courage. Someone needs your example. And yes, they even need to see you doing it scared, because that will give them permission to do the same.

So step out. Move forward. Take action. Do it scared. The world needs fearless leaders - not leaders who never feel scared, but leaders who refuse to let scared feelings stop them from being who God has called them to be and doing what God has called them to do. Your scared obedience today might be someone else's breakthrough tomorrow. Your trembling steps today might be someone else's trail map tomorrow.

This is your moment. This is your time. This is your season to rise up and be counted among those who felt scared but moved forward anyway. Don't wait for the fear to fully subside. Don't wait for perfect confidence. Don't wait for complete clarity. Move forward with what you have, where you are, as you are.

Because in the end, it's not about feeling fearless - it's about being faithful. It's not about being unafraid - it's about being unstoppable. It's not about never feeling scared - it's about never letting that scared feeling have the final word in your story.

So what the fear is going on? A new breed of leaders is rising - leaders who understand that being scared and being fearful are not the same thing. Leaders who are done letting fear write their story. Leaders who are ready to do it scared but do it anyway. And you, reading these words right now, are being called to join their ranks.

The only question that remains is this: Will you do it scared? Will you step out afraid? Will you move forward frightened? Because if you will, you'll discover what every great leader before you has discovered

– that on the other side of scared obedience lies supernatural outcome. On the other side of trembling trust lies tremendous triumph. On the other side of fearful faithfulness lies fantastic fulfillment.

Your next chapter awaits. Your next level calls. Your next assignment beckons. Do it scared, but be fearless. The world is waiting for what you carry, and it can't wait any longer for you to feel completely ready. The time is now. The person is you. The answer is yes.

Now go, and do it scared.

31 Prophetic Declarations for Fearless Leaders

1. I am not just called to leadership; I am anointed for fearless impact. My steps are ordered by the Lord, and my path is protected by His presence.
2. The spirit of fear has no authority in my life. I operate in power, love, and a sound mind in every decision I make.
3. I reject the chains of past failures. Today, I walk in the authority of one who learns from history but isn't bound by it.
4. My voice carries weight because it carries truth. I refuse to be silenced by intimidation or muted by opposition.
5. I am not bound by others' perceptions. I walk confidently in who God says I am, not who others think I should be.
6. Divine wisdom flows through my decision-making. I am led by the Spirit, not driven by fear or controlled by anxiety.
7. I break agreement with every generational spirit of fear. The bloodline curses of anxiety and doubt end with me.
8. My success doesn't threaten my relationships. I walk in both excellence and humility, influence and authenticity.
9. I am equipped for every challenge that comes with elevation. As my territory expands, my capacity increases.
10. The unknown doesn't paralyze me; it excites me. I embrace new territory with bold faith and confident expectation.

11. I am not afraid of standing alone. My conviction is not dependent on consensus, and my courage isn't tied to company.
12. Divine strategy flows through my leadership. I hear clearly, see accurately, and move precisely in every season.
13. I am not intimidated by others' gifts or achievements. I celebrate their success while confidently walking in my own lane.
14. The spirit of confusion has no place in my mind. I think with clarity, process with wisdom, and decide with confidence.
15. I am not afraid of correction or criticism. I embrace growth opportunities and transform challenges into stepping stones.
16. My past trauma does not define my future triumph. I am healed, whole, and walking in complete emotional freedom.
17. I break agreement with the spirit of comparison. I am fearlessly authentic, embracing my unique design and divine calling.
18. The spirit of rejection has no power over my decisions. I lead from acceptance in Christ, not the fear of man's approval.
19. I am not afraid of my own potential. I step fully into my greatness without apologizing for my God-given influence.
20. Divine acceleration marks my journey. I am not delayed by fear or detained by doubt; I move at heaven's pace.
21. I am not afraid to build what I haven't seen before. Innovation flows through my leadership, and creativity marks my path.
22. The spirit of inadequacy cannot limit my impact. I am fully equipped, divinely enabled, and perfectly positioned for this season.
23. I break agreement with spiritual intimidation. I walk in both authority and humility, power and grace, strength and wisdom.
24. My assignments are not aborted by fear. I carry every vision to completion, birth every mandate to maturity.
25. I am not afraid of outgrowing relationships. I honor my roots while embracing my wings, cherishing connection without limiting expansion.

26. Divine courage flows through my communication. I speak truth with love, confront issues with wisdom, and address challenges with grace.
27. The spirit of disappointment cannot control my expectations. I dream big, believe boldly, and advance confidently.
28. I am not afraid of being visible. I accept both the platform and the persecution, the influence and the opposition.
29. The anointing on my life makes room for me. I don't force doors open or manipulate opportunities; I walk through divine openings with confidence.
30. I break agreement with the poverty mindset. Fear of lack has no hold on my decisions; I operate in abundance mentality and kingdom prosperity.
31. I am a fearless steward of divine purpose. Everything God has deposited in me will achieve its intended impact, for His glory and kingdom advancement.

These declarations are more than words; they are weapons. They are not just affirmations; they are prophetic announcements. Speak them daily, believe them fully, walk in them confidently.

For they are not just declarations about what you do; They are declarations about who you are. Not just about your function; But about your identity.

Let them be the first words of your morning, The meditation of your day, The conviction of your heart, The foundation of your leadership.

For in declaring them, You are not just speaking about your future; You are speaking your future into being. You are not just describing who you want to become; You are becoming who you're declared to be.

Rise up, fearless leader. Declare your destiny. Speak your truth. Live your calling.

Fear not. Lead well. Impact greatly. Advance kingdom.

31 Questions for the Emerging Fearless Leader

1. What legitimate fears are you calling "humility" to avoid confronting your true potential?
2. In what areas of your leadership are you still trying to wear Saul's armor instead of embracing your own authentic style?
3. Which accomplishments are you downplaying to make others comfortable, and what impact is this having on those who need to see your example?
4. How is the fear of success causing you to negotiate your identity, and what parts of your authentic self are you trading for acceptance?
5. Like David with the lion, what is the "king of the jungle" in your life that, once defeated, will give you authority over lesser fears?
6. In what ways are you still leading from your molestation/trauma instead of your healing and transformation?
7. Where has isolation become an excuse for inaction rather than a season of preparation?
8. How are you handling being the first in your family to reach this level, and what generational fears are you still carrying?
9. What hidden seasons are you fighting against instead of embracing for your development?
10. Like Nehemiah, what internal fears are causing you to build walls instead of bridges in your leadership?
11. When was the last time you did something scared but did it anyway, and what did you learn about yourself in that moment?
12. What divine separation are you misinterpreting as demonic isolation?
13. Like Samuel with Saul, what or who are you still grieving that God has told you to let go of?
14. In what areas are you allowing the fear of others' perception to make you negotiate who God created you to be?
15. What successes are you minimizing because no one around you can relate to them?

16. How is the spirit of grief partnering with fear to keep you from moving forward in certain areas?
17. Like Elijah, are you believing you're alone in your assignment? How is this affecting your boldness?
18. What skills are you developing in your hidden season that seem unrelated to your calling but are actually preparing you?
19. Where has the fear of rejection caused you to create false humility instead of walking in true confidence?
20. What lions have you defeated that you're not giving yourself credit for, and how should those victories be affecting your current battles?
21. In what ways are you still allowing your family's perspective of you to limit your leadership capacity?
22. Like Joseph, how are you handling success that your family can't understand or celebrate?
23. What fears from your past season are you allowing to color your perception of your current opportunity?
24. How is the fear of losing relationship affecting your willingness to step into greater authority?
25. What tasks that seem menial (like Daniel-san waxing cars) are actually developing your leadership muscles?
26. Where has the fear of being seen caused you to hide gifts that others need to witness?
27. Like Gideon, what divine calling are you diminishing because of how you see yourself or your background?
28. What areas of success have become uncomfortable because you're the only one in your circle experiencing them?
29. How is the fear of outgrowing people influencing your willingness to grow?
30. What prophetic words or promises are you hesitating to step into because of fear of the unknown?
31. If fear wasn't a factor, what would you do in the next 30 days that would dramatically impact your destiny?

How to Use These Questions

These questions aren't just for quick answers. They're for deep reflection, journal exploration, and transformative action. For each question:

Take Time to Reflect:

- Sit with the question
- Journal your honest responses
- Identify patterns
- Recognize triggers
- Plan specific actions

Let Each Question:

- Challenge your assumptions
- Confront your fears
- Expose your excuses
- Reveal your potential
- Direct your growth

Use Them As:

- Morning meditations
- Journal prompts
- Prayer points
- Strategy sessions
- Growth markers

Remember:

- The goal isn't just answers
- The goal is awareness
- The goal is action
- The goal is transformation

Track Your Growth:

- Notice patterns
- Document insights
- Record breakthroughs
- Celebrate progress
- Plan next steps

Make This Personal: These questions aren't theoretical exercises; they're practical tools for transformation. Your honest answers can become the roadmap to your next level of fearless leadership.

Let them:

- Expose what needs exposure
- Heal what needs healing
- Break what needs breaking
- Build what needs building
- Release what needs releasing

Because your answers won't just reveal where you are; They'll help direct where you're going. They won't just show what you fear; They'll show what you're capable of.

Answer boldly. Reflect deeply. Act courageously. Lead fearlessly.

www.ingramcontent.com/pod-product-compliance
Lightning Source LLC
Chambersburg PA
CBHW060030110225
21714CB00013B/188